This book is dedicated to my wife, Bette, who has been my best friend for 60 years.

CUTTING THROUGH IT

CUTTING THROUGH IT

A SURGEON'S GUIDE TO SMARTER INVESTING

DR. RICHARD L. TREIMAN

ISBN 978-1-09831-337-1 eBook 978-1-09831-338-8

CONTENTS

FOREWORD

Throughout my 68 years in wealth management, it was my responsibility to help clients manage their investment portfolios and achieve their financial goals. I've been lucky enough to work with fascinating people, many of whom are leaders in their respective industries and professions. But in spite of how brilliant they may be, I was always surprised by how little some knew about investing and finance. How could it be that basic investing principles haven't become a part of common knowledge?

I've always had a personal interest in enhancing clients' understanding of investing and finance. Over the course of my career, I've combed through the instructional books written by some of the most successful investors of our time. But in spite of impressive author credits, I can't say that the knowledge within these books stuck with readers.

You can imagine my reluctance when I was asked to review a manuscript on investing written by a surgeon with no formal training in finance. The author was Dr. Richard Treiman, a highly-respected vascular surgeon in our community. Dr. Treiman was never a client; he personally managed his accounts and retirement funds from the day that he started his medical practice. As we started discussing his book, I quickly learned that he was no scrub. Not only had Dr. Treiman studied investors such as Benjamin Graham, Burton Malkiel, Howard Marks, Gerald Loeb, and Jeremy Siegel, he brought a unique perspective to the subject. Dr. Treiman wasn't like the other authors who had made careers out of managing exclusive funds. As a successful amateur investor, he had the ability to connect to people like my clients: regular men and women who didn't work on Wall Street.

To my surprise and enjoyment, I was taken by Dr. Treiman's manuscript. In the vast ocean of investing information, Dr. Treiman manages to pluck out the select material that a young investor needs to know. The book explains technical formulas and investing principles with crystal-clarity, often using engaging anecdotes and analogies to help the reader retain information. I'm impressed by the book's easy-to-read writing style, which held my interest. It's the very first book on investing that I can describe as a fun read.

If there's a single word to describe this book, it's "practical." Whether you're a student wanting to learn about investing, a young adult starting your career, or an established citizen who wants to seize control of your portfolio, this is the book for you. I only wish that Dr. Treiman could have written it 68 years earlier; it would have been my go-to referral for clients.

-Aaron Eshman

Former Senior Vice-President | Morgan Stanley Wealth Management
Past Governor | American Stock Exchange
Past Vice-Chairman | Pacific Stock Exchange
Past Member, Board of Directors | Security Industry Association

INTRODUCTION

About a year ago, my twelve-year-old grandson Jacob approached me after a family dinner.

"Grandpa, I have some money and want to buy a stock... what should I buy?" When I asked Jacob how he had acquired sufficient money to invest, he assured me that he'd saved every penny from birthdays and other holidays. I was impressed by that; his decision to forgo buying toys and games to save money for the future is the mentality of a real investor.

"I could tell you what I'm buying these days," I told him. "But I'm not sure it'll do you much good in the big picture."

"Why not?"

"Well, one stock might look good today...but how will you

know if it meets your expectations? And what about stocks that aren't good buys today but become profitable later?"

Jacob thought for a moment. "Can I ask for your help in the future?"

"I'll tell you what. Let me teach you the basics of investing, and then you won't need me at all. In time, maybe I'll be the one asking you for advice."

Jacob agreed, and I went to my office where I made notes on the fundamentals of common stocks and investing. Over the following weeks, I guided Jacob through the material, giving him review quizzes and hypothetical situations to navigate. It wasn't long before I was scouring Amazon to find a book on investing that would take Jacob's education to the next level. I was surprised to find that among the sea of books on the subject, very few approach the material from an amateur's perspective. Most titles are written by financial experts who manage hedge funds. But these qualifications don't make them particularly good at leveling with a novice to the investing world.

I ended up purchasing what seemed to be the most accessible book that I could find, but Jacob scarcely made it through the first chapter. The book enforced an all-too popular fallacy: investing is dense, boring, and reserved for people in fancy suits.

This fallacy is nothing new. It affected me when I was barely making ends meet as a young doctor. Though I'd served in the Navy, made it through medical school, and gotten married, I barely knew the difference between a common stock portfolio and a mutual fund. As I was toiling away at my medical practice, I remember hearing friends and colleagues talking about the stock market and their investments. These conversations intimidated me, quite frankly. Why? I wasn't afraid of tackling a complex surgery or changing my kids' diapers. But for some reason, investing was a grizzly bear that I didn't want to confront.

Over the course of my life, I've found that I'm not the only one who felt this way. The average Joes and Janes don't miss out on investing because it's difficult...they miss out on investing because it's daunting. We seem to share a universal fear of investing that feeds on our ignorance of the subject. It really isn't our fault; courses on financial health aren't a part of high school curriculums. That lends itself to quite a bit of confusion over the various types of securities, the risks of investing, the strategy used to evaluate stocks, and the process of using investments to fund retirement.

If it wasn't for hearing about investing from my colleagues in the hospital, I probably would have never gotten involved in investing. But I suppose that peer pressure can be a good thing; I educated myself and built an investment portfolio that ultimately bankrolled my retirement. I say this not for the sake of indulgence, but to make a point: it's never too late to get started, and you don't need to be a wolf of Wall Street to succeed as an investor. Though it's easy to throw up your hands and pretend that you've missed the investing boat, that simply isn't true. Whether you're nineteen or ninety-one, you can benefit from the stock market if you commit to gaining foundational knowledge.

The goal of this book is to provide you with the tools that are necessary for building a profitable investment portfolio. Using the notes that I prepared for Jacob as an outline, I've covered not only the essentials of investing, but specific strategies that will lead to financial success over the long-term. Everything that you need to know to become a successful investor is covered in nine accessible chapters. After each chapter, I've included "The Bullet Points" that summarize the lessons in bite-sized sentences. Here's what we'll cover.

Chapter 1: The Meat & Potatoes of Common Stocks

In this chapter, I provide an overview of the world of common stocks. I'll answer key questions, such as:

- What's a common stock?
- What do you own when you buy a stock?
- What's your responsibility as a stockholder?
- How are stocks priced?
- How are stocks bought and sold?
- Why should you start investing in common stocks over other forms of investment?

I also confront inflation and the Federal Reserve, the two macroeconomic factors that have a broad impact on your savings and investments. The chapter also covers exchange-traded funds (ETFs) and index funds. We'll specifically get into the S&P 500 and the Dow Jones Industrial Average, which are used as an index of the stock market as a whole.

Chapter 2: The Mentality of a Successful Investor

Here, I'll explain the mindset that generally leads to success in the investing world. After hedging the importance of sound budgeting and constantly observing the market, I'll unveil the big secret that will lead to financial stability: long-term investing. To help you develop your own investing strategy, I'll introduce you to philosophies developed by well-recognized experts such as Benjamin Graham, Peter Lynch, Warren Buffet, and others.

Chapter 3: How to Choose a Common Stock

Chapter 3 is where we dive deep into the nuts and bolts of investing. These pages will teach you how to find key stocks that are worth investing in. We'll tackle seemingly daunting metrics, enabling you to properly evaluate a stock. We'll also look under the hood at a company's financials by diving into balance sheets, cash flow statements, and income statements. I know that you're not an accountant and neither am I, but there's valuable information in these reports that can justify buying or passing on a given stock. Once you understand these terms, you'll rise to the head of the class and be the envy of your colleagues.

Computers can spit out reams of calculations about a stock,

and we'll jump straight to the ones that matter most: the 52-week high and low, P/E Ratio, Book Value Per Share, Dividends & Yield, and Return on Equity. I'll show you how these are calculated using simple numbers and basic arithmetic, which will prepare you to fully master these concepts.

Chapter 4: Lessons from the Pit

In Chapter 4, I'll lay out my personal successes and failures that stand out over the course of my 50+ years of investing . My hope is that by evaluating what went right and what went wrong in my portfolio, you'll be able to repeat my successes and avoid my failures.

Chapter 5: General Upkeep: Building a Boat to Last

Finding good stocks is only half the battle; another major part of investing involves looking after the health of your portfolio. Chapter 5 will teach you how to keep your investment portfolio up-to-date. I'll introduce you to strategies that will boost your investment results such as dividend reinvestment programs, dollar averaging, and investment clubs. These tools will ensure that your portfolio continues to work for you.

I'll also discuss the strategy of cashing out on stocks. At first glance, selling stocks seems like the best part of investing, as it corresponds to money in the bank. But without the proper guidance, selling stocks can be confusing and even stressful. Without violating our commitment to long-term investing,

Chapter 5 will teach you how to determine when to sell a stock.

Chapter 6: Stocks of a Different Breed

The bulk of this book is dedicated to common stocks, exchange traded funds, and index funds, but there are many additional investments that you should incorporate into your portfolio as you get older. Chapter 6 will introduce you to worthwhile opportunities that will turn you into a well-rounded investor.

Chapter 7: The Value of Fixed Income Securities

Like the chapter before it, Chapter 7 is designed to open your eyes to additional types of investments. These pages, however, focus on fixed-income securities that can safeguard you from volatility in the market. This discussion on bonds, treasuries and CDs will help you create a stable portfolio for your future.

Chapter 8: Taxes & Accounts: Your Burden & Your Buckets

Taxes are never a joy to talk about, but they play a major role in one's investment strategy. Here, I'll explain how taxes affect you specifically and suggest ways to minimize tax liabilities.

I'll also tackle the question of how to sort your finances with different accounts. It might seem like all money is created equal, but that's not the case. If you want to optimize your investments, you need to have a solid understanding of how to divvy up your wealth among your accounts.

Chapter 9: Setting the Table for your Future

While investing is tremendously valuable to one's financial well-being, it comes with its share of threats and challenges. The final chapter of this book will identify the monsters of investing and discuss the six bear markets in recent memory, preparing you for future dips in the market. We'll also discuss the "Ideal Portfolio," as subjective a term as that is, leaving you with a clear direction in your investing career.

As you can see, the book covers a wealth of material. I don't expect you to read it through in one sitting; in fact, I don't want you to: it's too much to absorb. Rather, take one chapter at a time and be sure you understand the concepts before moving on to the next chunk of material. But if there's one word to describe this book, it's 'practical'; every sentence is designed to help you succeed as a novice investor.

Throughout the text, I've highlighted key terms that are included in a glossary at the end of the book. As a student of investing myself, I know how difficult it is to retain all of this knowledge, and I've done my best to present this information in an accessible way. My goal is not just to introduce you to the world of investing, but to empower you to apply this knowledge in the real world. Doing so may give you the financial freedom that you've always wanted.

Throughout the book, I share some of my opinions on investments that I deem attractive. These thoughts should not be construed as assurances, as there are risks associated with all investments. However, it should be noted that each recommendation was formulated during the writing of this manuscript: the years 2018-2019.

I ask one thing from the reader before we get started. If you can, cast aside any negative thoughts you may have about stocks and investing. The subject of investing has a somewhat poor reputation for being bland and inaccessible, when it's really just the opposite. It's my goal to convince you that investing is not a necessary evil. It can actually be fun.

Enough chit chat — let's get started making you a successful investor.

1

THE MEAT & POTATOES OF COMMON STOCKS

Think about how much time you've dedicated to math throughout your life. Though American students typically begin their math education in the 1st grade, things don't really get cooking until the 3rd grade when the curriculum invokes the dreaded multiplication tables. Let's do some math of our own — if the average student devotes an hour of every school day to math, he or she will spend 180 hours per year. That routine continues for a full decade, from 3rd to 12th grade, putting us at 1,800 hours of math in total. This is a conservative estimate, as students in advanced courses probably spend far more than an hour per day crunching numbers.

Now, compare those hours to the little or no time allotted to studying investing or developing skills that are vital for financial success. It's no wonder that we get intimidated when we hear terms like "Price/Earnings Ratio" or "dividend reinvestment strategy." It isn't because those concepts are particularly challenging; it's because we don't have a foundational knowledge of them.

This chapter is designed to give you a basic knowledge of investment terminology and concepts. Consider this a crash course in basic stocks; we're cramming quite a bit of information into a short space. My purpose here is not to provide definitive knowledge of stocks and trading. Rather, my goal is to provide you with practical information that you'll need to succeed as an amateur investor.

If you already have mastery of a certain concept, feel free to flip ahead to the next section. But if your understanding is shaky, it may be worth reading through these basic concepts. If you don't have a sound vocabulary, you're bound to hit some bumps down the road.

/

What's a Common Stock?

What do you own when you buy a stock? First and foremost, let's clarify the term — when people use the term "stock," they're actually referring to common stocks, which are the majority of items listed on the stock exchanges. Preferred stocks are a separate beast that operate differently — more on those later on. Purchasing a common stock means that you own a share of a public company. When I say public, or publicly-owned, I mean that the company doesn't have a single owner. Rather, it's co-owned by the thousands, tens of thousands, or even millions of people who buy stock in the company.

While it's also possible to invest in a privately-owned company — that is, a company that's owned by a select number of people — you can't do so by buying stocks. For the scope of this book, we're going to exclude talking about investing in private companies. Private investments typically require more money, a heightened level of risk, and a sophisticated knowledge of finance. Let's leave investing in private companies to the professional investors.

Why is it advantageous for a company to be public as opposed to privately-owned? Like most things, it all comes down to money. Private companies rely on owners and investors to pump money, or capital, into the business. Because there are less people involved, there's less capital available to the company. Public companies raise far more capital than private companies by enabling everyone to buy shares of stock.

Let's look at Tesla as an example. It's safe to say that creating a new fleet of electric supercars is a lofty goal, and lofty goals require cash. While the CEO Elon Musk has billions of dollars that he could potentially invest in the company, his wealth alone isn't enough to support a company of Tesla's scale. More, it would be irresponsible for Musk to risk his financial livelihood on a single business. To raise the capital required to pay employees, develop new automotive technologies, and manufacture their vehicles, Tesla went public. As of June of

2019, Tesla has sold 177 million shares of stock, with the price of each share dipping to prices around $150/share and rising to prices around $350/share. If we pick a middle number of $250/share, we can see how much capital has been raised by making the company public:

$250 (price per share) × 177,000,000 (number of shares) = **$44.25 billion dollars.** That's a lot of dough.

Shares Outstanding

If stocks correspond to ownership in a company, how many shares of stock are available at any given time? As expected, the answer varies with respect to the company and the market. When a company "goes public" — that is, turns its ownership over to the general populace who can buy stocks in the company, it issues a number of shares, often in the hundreds of millions. Of the shares issued, a relatively small number are held in the company's treasury for possible acquisitions and executive pay. The majority are released for trading and are called shares outstanding (aka "the float").

Why Should I Invest in Common Stocks?

There are several reasons why common stocks are attractive to the novice investor. Let's review them.

1) Stocks don't require tons of money to get started.

Out of all the different types of investments, stocks are the most accessible to the general public. That's because you can start investing in the stock market without having tons of capital. In order to invest in something like a private company or real estate, you would need quite a bit of money to get your foot in the door. But with the stock market, you can start investing with any sum of money, no matter how small.

2) Stocks have a high ceiling for profit.

Telling you that you're bound to make money in the stock market is akin to promising you a good job after receiving a college education. While I'd be remiss in making such a broad generalization, investing in common stocks opens the door to financial success. Common stocks also happen to be far more profitable than many other investment types. A number of studies have shown that over the long-term, stocks outperform fixed income securities like bonds and treasuries. We'll get into those types of investments later.

3) There's no bargaining with stock prices.

When you're an amateur in a big sea of industry professionals, it's easy to get the short end of the stick. The great thing about stocks is that everyone pays the same price and there's no bargaining whatsoever. While it's certainly possible to make bad decisions in the stock market, you can rest assured that you aren't getting fleeced on any transaction.

4) Common stocks can be sold at any time.

Investing in common stocks is a liquid investment; that is, it can be sold for cash at any moment. Buying and selling stocks is remarkably quick and easy — all you need is a brokerage account and access to a computer. Other investments can be much more difficult to sell. For example, owning a piece of real estate or a work of fine art is only worthwhile if there's a willing buyer, and there is always negotiation on price.

5) If you exhibit a long-term investing strategy, you can safeguard yourself against volatility.

My job isn't to become a cheerleader for common stocks; it's to give you a foundation for investment success. Thus, it's key that I acknowledge the biggest downside to common stocks: volatility and risk. You can lessen risk by becoming a long-term investor. From a statistical perspective, it's inevitable that the value of your stocks will decrease when the stock market dips. This should not dissuade you from investing in stocks! History has shown that the market is undefeated; overall, it's on a steady climb. By being a long-term investor — that is, committing to your investments and staying in the market for years on end — temporary dips in the stock market will not affect your long-term goal.

The Risks of Investing & Diversification

The financial guru Howard Marks wrote that because no one knows the future, understanding risk is the most essential element in becoming a successful investor. The most obvious risk relates to the fact that we can't guarantee a return on our investments. Whenever we put money into a stock or a fund, we have to accept the possibility that the investment will go underwater.

While we can't eliminate risk, we can lessen it through a strategy called diversification. Having a diversified portfolio means that your portfolio consists of different stocks, index funds, and exchange traded funds (ETFs) in a variety of economic sectors. Having a diversified portfolio is like having a ship with anti-sinking technology. All of the Navy's ships are made with several air-tight compartments that can take on water without the whole ship going under. That means that if a torpedo hits one part of the vessel, the ship can keep on sailing. Your portfolio should operate the exact same way. By making multiple investments in different industries, a single downturn won't sink your portfolio.

When you're buying common stocks, don't just look for one or two 'hot' industries. Doing so will make you vulnerable to swift changes in the market. Instead, you should aim to diversify your holdings into a variety of different economic sectors. The stock market is divided into 11 sectors:

- Energy
- Basic Materials
- Industrials
- Consumer Discretionary
- Consumer Stables
- Healthcare
- Financials
- Technology

- Communication
- Utilities
- Real Estate

As you follow the market, you'll notice that economic sectors rarely act the same way. This means that your stable holdings will offset the losses endured by other investments.

As you grow older, you should apply the principles of diversification to incorporate different types of investments beyond common stocks. Buying stocks should be your initial investment, but you don't want to put all your eggs in one basket; baskets can break. Chapters 6 and 7 have necessary information on other types of securities that can further protect your portfolio from risk.

The Bugaboo of Inflation

As investors, we all have the common goal of growing our wealth. In order to achieve that, we need to understand the forces that are working against us. The biggest culprit is inflation, which is the ongoing loss of the buying power of money over time. Inflation means that a single item in the economy will cost increasingly more as time progresses. Put another way, your money is guaranteed to lose its value. As an example, if something costs $100 today, the same item might cost $103 next year, $107 the following year, and $111 the year after that. If your investment fund is a swimmer cutting through the ocean, inflation is the current that's working against him. The swimmer must overcome the forces of inflation in order to go a certain distance.

Inflation is just like aging — it often goes unnoticed because of its gradual nature. I'll give you an example; for one reason or another, I've kept each of my driver's licenses since the DMV first issued me a license. When I have to take a new license photograph, I don't feel like I've aged since my last visit to the DMV. But if you look at all of the photographs in a row, you can see my face transforming with age. The same thing goes for inflation, and it's just as annoying as getting older. From one year to the next, the average citizen probably doesn't feel the weight of inflation. A five-cent increase for a cup of coffee probably isn't going to keep the average customer awake at night. But as investors, we have to train ourselves to think about long-term effects. Just as every child turns into a senior citizen, inflation will weaken the power of the dollar.

The inflation rate is what you'd expect it to be: the percent increase of the cost of a good or service from one year to the next. For example, let's say that a pair of shoes costs $80 this year, and the inflation rate is 2.4%. To calculate what it will cost next year, we can do some basic arithmetic:

$$\$80 \times .024 = \$1.92$$

$$\$80 + \$1.92 = \mathbf{\$81.92}$$

One statistic used to determine the inflation rate is the Consumer Price Index (CPI). The CPI is essentially a record of changing costs for goods and services used in daily living. For practical purposes, you can consider the CPI to be about the same as the inflation rate.

The government monitors the inflation rate based on a number of factors such as money supply, productivity, wages, and a host of other variables that the individual investor cannot control. The annual inflation rate is published every year.

If you aren't convinced that inflation is worthy of consideration, look to the case of Germany after World War I. After the Allies declared victory over the Axis Powers in 1918, Germany was ordered to pay massive reparations (think of reparations like a traffic fine on steroids). It goes without saying that the German government wasn't happy about this, but what choice did they have? They had just gotten their tails handed to them by the Allies. The economists of the new German government tried to skirt the reparation problem by printing more units of German money, which they could then use to buy foreign currency. Sounds good in theory, right? Unfortunately for Germany, it didn't work out.

By printing vast amounts of money, Germany massively reduced the value of their own currency. In early 1922, one U.S. dollar was equal to 320 German marks, the mark being the unit of Germany currency. In other words, the German economy was struggling in relation to foreign markets. But that was just the beginning of Germany's inflation problems.

As the reparations forced the treasury to continue printing more money, the value of the mark dropped like an anvil. By the end of 1922, the cost of a loaf of bread ballooned from 160 to 200,000,000,000 German marks. By November of the following year, one U.S. dollar was worth 4,210,500,000,000 German marks. In other words, German currency had about the same value as a dirt clod. It didn't matter if you were a billionaire, a trillionaire, or a quadrillionaire; if you were beholden to the German economy, you were broke. Home-owners used paper bills to cover their walls because they couldn't afford wallpaper. Kids played with stacks of bills instead of legos because they couldn't afford toys. Thousands of families started burning their cash because they couldn't afford firewood.

Hopefully (knock on wood), we'll never experience something as devastating as German hyperinflation. But regardless of how stable our economy is, inflation will always play a role. That means that we have to account for it in our investment plans.

If you've learned about swings in the market — the stock market crash of 1929, the recession of 2007 — you may think that the safest way to preserve your money is to put it into a savings account. Oddly enough, that isn't the case! Savings accounts are good to have as a fund that you can draw from for daily expenses, but any financial adviser will tell you that they aren't a good way to build wealth for your future. Why? The interest that you earn from a savings account tends to be less than the inflation rate.

For example, if you have $1,000 dollars in a savings account that earns 1% annual interest, you'll make $10 each year that you have the account. However, if the annual inflation rate is 2%, the cost of items that you need to buy is increasing faster than the money in your savings. In this scenario, you're effectively losing 1% of your money each year. To compensate for the eroding power of inflation, you must invest in something that grows your wealth faster than inflation renders it moot. With the annual inflation rate around 2%, your annual yield must reach this number in order to break even.

How are Stocks Priced?

If you walk into a store to go shopping — let's say you're in need of a jacket — you'll notice that the store has a fixed price on every item of inventory. Whatever the number on the price tag may be, it's held constant and not subject to change. In addition to having power over the price, the store gets to determine how many jackets they want to buy from the manufacturer. Assuming that the manufacturer had unlimited resources, the store could technically buy an infinite number of jackets to resell to the consumer.

Stocks don't work this way. First of all, there are a finite number of shares issued by a company, often in the millions. Secondly, the price of a stock is never fixed. Rather, the price is determined by how well the company is doing at a particular moment in time and how well the company is projected to do in the future. For example, the stock price of a struggling company could shoot up if it gets a huge influx of orders or if the market changes to better suit the company. At any given time, the buyers and sellers of a stock determine that stock's price. People are constantly buying and selling shares of a given stock, and the price of each share fluctuates depending on two factors: the Ask Price, or how much the seller wants to sell the shares for; and the Bid Price, or how much the buyer is willing to purchase the shares. If there are more buyers than sellers for a given stock, the price will rise. Conversely, if there are more sellers than buyers, the price will fall.

If the selling of jackets operated on the same basis as the stock market, there would be a set number of jackets available. It would be impossible to manufacture an additional jacket, and it would be impossible to destroy an existing jacket. The jackets would not be purchased from a store; they would change hands from one person to another. In the cold months, the price of the jacket would increase, and in the summer months it would drop.

You may notice that this model sounds much more like trading than buying: hence the commonly-used term "stock market trading."

How are Stocks Bought & Sold?

Common stocks aren't like groceries; you can't go out and buy them at a store. Stocks are bought and sold primarily through two markets, or stock exchanges:

- The New York Stock Exchange (NYSE)
- The NASDAQ Stock Exchange (NASDAQ)

Of course there are exceptions to this — some companies trade stocks using other stock exchanges, and there are stock exchanges in other countries. However, the NYSE and the NASDAQ are the only relevant entities for the novice investor. There are over 5,000 companies listed on these two exchanges, and millions of shares are traded each day. In other words, there isn't a shortage of decisions to be made when it comes to choosing a stock. Whenever a public company becomes available on one of these stock exchanges, they receive a letter abbreviation. For instance, AMZN is designated to Amazon, AAPL to Apple, and COST to Costco.

A teaspoon of history for you: the concept of stock exchanges extends all the way back to the East India Company, which operated in 1602. The NYSE is a bit younger, founded in 1792, and the NASDAQ kicked off in 1971 when a number of smaller exchanges combined into a single entity. If you've ever wondered why people refer to the investing world as Wall Street, it's because the NYSE is located at 11 Wall Street in New York City.

Now a trivia question: can you guess the origin of the term "stock exchange"? Hundreds of years ago, domestic animals called livestock were housed in pens prior to being bought or sold. The areas where the animals were traded came to be known as "stock exchanges." This concept evolved into more modern stock exchanges, where people traded shares of companies instead of animals. Today, things are far more sophisticated; all sales are conducted electronically using computers. The concept of stock exchanges ultimately evolved from trading animals to trading all kinds of things, including companies. There you go — a fun fact to fill the silence at your next awkward family dinner.

While stocks are the most common listings on the NYSE and the NASDAQ, an investor can also buy other types of funds as well. All purchases and sales must be conducted while the stock exchanges are open, which is from 9:30 AM to 4:00 PM Eastern Time on Mondays through Fridays (excluding holidays). Since stock exchanges are the entities through which stocks are bought and sold, you might think that you can buy shares from them directly — however, that isn't the case. Rather, the individual needs to use a brokerage house or brokerage, a 'middle-man' business that has a relationship with the stock exchanges. Unfortunately, all brokerage houses charge a commission on every stock transaction that you make. Let's discuss the different types of brokerage houses that you can use.

Discount Brokerages

Discount brokerages are the more hands-on option, which allow you to do your own buying and selling. While the commission fees are subject to vary, you can expect to pay between five and ten dollars for each transaction through a discount brokerage.

Full-Service Brokerages

Full-service brokerages are like full-service gasoline stations; an employee will pump your gas instead of you having to do it yourself. As you can expect, the commission from a full-service brokerage will be considerably higher than that of a discount brokerage. It's impossible to provide an accurate estimate for commissions, as it varies on a number of factors (the number of shares being traded, the price of each share, etc). Expect to pay no less than fifty or sixty dollars if you go with a full-service brokerage.

Aside from convenience, are you getting anything from a full-service brokerage? The answer is a resounding yes. Using a full-service brokerage means getting access to a broker that you can call and discuss possible investments. These brokerage houses also have research departments that can offer valuable insight into individual stocks and different types of investments. A good full-service broker will keep an eye on your portfolio and call you with major updates on your stocks. Overall, you're buying an investment pal with whom you can huddle up and discuss strategy.

Discount or Full-Service — which one's right for me?

While this is the right question to be asking, it really depends on the situation. It can be scary to use a discount brokerage when you're new to the stock market and have limited experience. That being said, you don't want to pay high commissions if you aren't getting value from your full-service brokerage, and you can imagine that the quality of brokerage houses can range pretty widely.

If you're hellbent on finding your own stocks and making your own decisions, use a discount brokerage. For instance, many young investors are bound to gravitate towards the stable giants of the market — companies like Amazon, Apple, and Google. It doesn't take a savvy broker to tell you that these are valuable stocks, so I probably wouldn't pay a hefty commission for those transactions. But if you're on the lookout for exciting stocks that fall under the radar, try scouting for a reputable full-service brokerage with reasonable commissions.

Bids, Asks, and Limit Orders

Because the price of a stock is always changing, it's important to be discerning about the current price before making a purchase. Let's say that you need to buy new running shoes. You probably have a pretty strong idea of what you're going to spend — somewhere between seventy-five and one hundred dollars. Sure, you might walk into a doorbuster sale and get a pair for cheap, but the price of the shoes is largely set. Waiting for the price to drop won't do you much good.

By contrast, the price of a stock is far more volatile. That means you might establish a firm number of what you think the stock is worth before making a purchase. You can do this by making a bid on a certain stock — that is, the amount that you're willing to pay for one share. The bid is always held in relation to the ask, which is the amount that the stock is currently going for. If your bid is the same price as the ask, go ahead and buy the stock.

I should note that most transactions are pretty simple, as the difference between the bid and ask is typically small in relation to the price of the stock. If you're purchasing through a discount brokerage, you would execute the process by logging into your account on a computer and indicating the stock of interest, as well as the number of shares you'd like to buy. Then, you will place an order to buy "at the market," which is the best price that the brokerage can get for you. The transaction is typically completed within a matter of seconds. If you happen to be using a full-service brokerage, the process is even easier; you simply contact your brokerage house, indicate the relevant information, and they will handle the rest.

However, over the course of your investing career, you may find yourself sniffing at an interesting stock that you think is too expensive. Rather than constantly checking the market to see if the stock price has dropped so that you can make a purchase, you can set something called a limit order. This is essentially an order that stipulates a set price that you're willing to pay for a given stock.

For example, let's say a stock for an exciting new tech company — let's call it ABC — is trading for $30 per share. You like what you see in the company, but you only think the stock is worth $25 per share. Through your discount or full-service brokerage, you can place a limit order for $25 on any number of shares. For the sake of example, let's say that you want to buy 10 shares of stock. In a week, the hype behind the ABC companies dies down, and the stock price drops to $25 per share. Without you having to do a single thing, the brokerage will automatically process your limit order, purchasing 10 shares of stock for you and taking $250 out of your account. Now, let's say that after being priced at $30 per share, ABC announces a great new product and the stock price shoots up. If you set your limit order at $25, your order will not be processed.

You can also place a limit order to sell a given stock at a set price. These operate the exact same way, except rather than waiting for a stock price to drop, you would be waiting for a stock price to rise so that you can sell at your price. The cool thing about limit orders is that you can set the term during which it remains valid. A limit order can be good for a single day, or it can be good until you decide to cancel it. Limit orders can be tremendously advantageous because they keep you from having to obsess over fluctuating prices in the market.

Being a Shareholder: Your Role and Your Responsibility

Let's say that you buy a single share of Tesla stock. Congratulations! You're technically a part owner of the company. However, the title is often far fancier than it sounds. Because companies issue so many shares of their stock, owning a single share gives you negligible control over the company. In the olden days, every stock purchase was documented with a paper certificate, but you can imagine how many trees that killed. Today, stock ownership is recorded electronically. It goes without saying that you can own any number of stocks. If you happen to acquire stock shares in more than a single company, you have a portfolio of stocks.

I wish that I could tell you that you can disregard the inner-workings of the companies in which you invest, but doing so would be a disservice to you. Once you become a shareholder in a company, you're hitching your financial success to that of the company in question. That means that you should stay informed on the business' performance. You might not have the power to make the company succeed, but you have the power of your investment.

Proposals and Proxy Battles

When you buy a stock and become an owner, you'll be invited to the company's annual meeting. Here, the share-holders are allowed to vote on proposals, or important topics such as membership on the Board of Directors and other matters that probably matter very little to you. All proposals to be voted upon at the annual meeting are sent to share-holders beforehand. In addition, it's your right as a share-holder to submit your own proposal for a change to the company's business practice, which would be voted upon at the annual meeting. All proposals must be submitted prior to the annual meeting.

If you're anything like me, you won't attend these annual meetings because they're inconvenient and arduous. Moreover, you can electronically vote on proposals without attending the annual meeting — instructions for doing so will be sent to you by the company. If you decide to exercise your right to vote, you're entitled to one vote for each share of the company that you own. I hate to be the bearer of bad news, but it's worth noting that unless you have a heaping number of shares in a stock (which is not wise if you want a balanced portfolio), your votes won't have any impact on an issue.

On rare occasions, the company will enter a proxy battle for seats on the Board of Directors. A proxy battle occurs when a group holding a lot of shares wants to change how the company is run. If a proxy battle occurs, you will receive two sets of ballots: one for each side asking for your vote. You might even receive a phone call urging you to vote one way or the other. If you think that your company has the potential of being crippled by poor management, the outcome of these proxy battles may play a role in you keeping or selling a stock. But for the most part, these are of very little importance to you.

Annual Reports

As a shareholder, you will receive, or can request, an annual report. The report includes reams of financial information, most of which will be beyond your understanding or interest. However, there's a diamond in the rough amidst this documentation. If you scour the table of contents of your annual report, you'll find a "report to the shareholders," which is written by the President or Chief Executive Officer (CEO).

This letter discusses the company's past year's performance and its plans for the future. I advise you to read this report, as it will provide pointed information regarding the health of the company. Being written by the CEO, the report will certainly focus on the good and minimize the bad; however, you should be able to detect if the company is struggling. Keep an eye out for key phrases like "restructuring" and "taking advantage of new opportunities." These are 'red flags' and indicate that the company may have seen better days.

If a company restructures, I encourage you to review the fundamentals of the company to see if you want to hold or sell your stock. That being said, not all restructuring is a bad thing; it's a common occurrence when one company takes over another business.

The Federal Reserve and the Stock Market

Once you begin investing, you'll start following the state of the economy as a whole. In conversation, you'll find that people classify the market as one of two states. A bull market occurs when the economy is hot and the prices of stocks are rising. A bear market is just the opposite, kicking in when the market is trending downwards.

Why these odd names? Bull markets are called as such because bulls fight with their horns turned up. Bears, on the other hand, fight with their paws turned downwards — hence, the correlation to down markets. Who wins the fight, you may ask? The bull. While bear markets are sprinkled throughout the history of the economy, the market is always trending in a generally positive direction over time.

As you gain more experience, you'll notice an undeniable trend between the health of the market and the price of your stocks. The price of stocks typically moves in the same direction as the collective market. Thus the saying, "a rising tide raises all boats."

This is because the market tries to anticipate the health of the overall economy. As the economy is expected to expand, stock prices rise; as the economy shows signs of vulnerability, stock prices drop. Because you will be a long-term investor, movements of the stock market over months or even years should not influence your investment plan. Nonetheless, it's only natural that you'll keep a careful eye on the market once you invest.

Out of the numerous factors that impact the economy and the market, the one that deserves the most attention is the Federal Reserve, often referred to as The Fed. The Federal Reserve is the banking system of the United States. One of its functions is to keep the economy on an even keel. The Fed can accomplish that by monitoring two factors: monetary policy and the Federal Funds Rate. If the economy starts to lag, the Fed will add stimuli by putting more money into the economy and lowering the Federal Funds Rate. Conversely, if the economy becomes overheated and inflation raises its ugly head, the Fed will withdraw money from the economy and raise the Federal Funds Rate. Let's dive into how this works.

Monetary Policy

The Fed's monetary policy determines the amount of money in circulation. When there's more money in the economy, the following tends to occur:

- People spend more on goods and services
- Prices increase
- Businesses make more money
- Stocks rise

All of these are good things, right? The one caveat is that if there's too much money in circulation, the economy is at risk for inflation. For that reason, the Fed will create policies that decrease the amount of money in circulation. This is a necessary evil to keep inflation in check; when it happens, you can expect the economy to contract and stock values to drop.

Federal Funds Rate

The Federal Funds Rate determines the interest rates that banks charge each other for overnight or short-term loans. Why is this important? Well, the Federal Funds Rate has a direct impact on interest rates that the consumer pays on any type of loan. That includes mortgages on a home, student loans, and car loans. For the most part, we can expect the following:

When the Federal Fund Rate is low:

- Interest rates drop
- Money managers put their clients' money into stocks over fixed-income securities
- People borrow more money from banks
- Companies borrow more money from banks, which they use to expand business
- The market thrives

When the Federal Funds Rate is high:

- Interest rates rise
- Money managers put their clients' money into fixed-income securities over stocks
- People pull back on borrowing
- Company expansion slows, as businesses enter 'survival mode'
- The market weakens

We can't do anything to affect the actions of The Fed, but it's important to understand its actions as we make investing decisions. You make money when your stock appreciates in value; that means that you want to buy when prices are low. If the Fed is pumping tons of money into the market and mandates a low Federal Funds Rate, it may not be the time to invest because stock prices will be very high.

Exchange Traded Funds (ETFs) and Index Funds

Rather than investing in a single company, you can buy one stock that includes a basket of companies doing a similar kind of business; or one stock that tracks an index of the market. Although technically similar, I refer to the former as an exchange traded fund (ETF) and the latter as an index fund.

If a common stock is a particular vegetable (let's say a tomato plant), ETFs are the whole garden. In a given season, it's possible that tomatoes become the fastest growing plant. But it's also possible that tomatoes have a tough year and the zucchinis and carrots take off. In that case, you want to be investing not just in tomatoes, but in the growth of the garden as a whole. In short, ETFs allow you to invest in a given sector of the economy without the risk of investing in a single company. I suggest selecting ETFs that include major companies doing a similar kind of business. That could include utilities, energy, financials, technology, consumer staples, materials, and other segments of the economy.

Index funds operate on the same principles as ETFs, as they offset risk by sprinkling your investment over a variety of companies. However, the companies in an index fund aren't necessarily determined by a common industry like ETFs. Index funds track the value of the market as a whole. In other words, if you buy a share of an index fund, the price of your share will go up and down approximately the same percent as the collective market.

In Chapter 3, which will guide you through the criteria for selecting individual investments, my goal is to provide you with a toolkit that enables you to make strategic decisions for the rest of your investing career. However, I kick the chapter off by recommending two index funds that should serve as the pillars of your portfolio: the S&P 500, and the Dow Jones Industrial Average Fund. We'll talk about why later.

A Summation of the Market: The Dow Jones Industrial Average

The Dow Jones Industrial Average (DJIA), often referred to as "The Dow," is a measure of how well the stock market is doing on any given day. If someone asks, "What did the market do today," they are asking if the DJIA went up or down. The DJIA began in 1896 when two financial reporters, Charles Dow and Edward Jones, averaged the prices of twelve industrial stocks as a sample for the market. The DJIA was later enlarged to 30 companies, some of which were non-industrial. Since its inception over one hundred years ago, the 30 component companies that make up the DJIA have been changed fifty-four times. This "changing of the guard" has occurred when new economic powerhouses such as Apple, IBM, and Walmart come along and prior giants such as Sears, General Electric, and Bethlehem Steel lose their way.

The Pillars of Your Portfolio: The Dow Jones Industrial Average Fund (DIA) and the S&P 500 (SPY)

This book is designed to give you the framework to make smart investing decisions — not to recommend particular investments. That being said, I'm about to break that rule. Prepare yourself for the most direct and clear advice that I would give to any investor.

Invest in the SPY and DIA index funds. These should serve as the backbone of your portfolio.

The S&P 500 fund (symbol SPY, commonly referred to as 'Spiders'); and the Dow Industrial Average fund (symbol DIA, commonly referred to as 'Diamonds') are the two best known funds that you can buy. The S&P 500 gets the first half of its name from the Standard and Poor's Financial Company, which averages and reports the data on a daily basis; and the second half of its name from the number of companies that make up the fund: 500. Created in 1993, the S&P 500 was one of the first index funds, and it's one of the largest ones in existence. The DIA fund is just as reputable as the S&P 500. Collectively, the SPY and DIA funds are often referred to as "the market." If you take a magnifying glass to the fine print, these are trusts that are commonly referred to as funds. For practical purposes, they act exactly like a stock fund. By owning a share of either of these funds, your investment will be tied to the collective stock market.

Now, all ETFs and index funds have a cost of doing business, which is deducted from the assets of the fund each year, regardless of the performance of the fund. That cost is called an expense ratio. The expense ratios for the SPY and DIA funds hover around 0.09% and 0.16%, respectively. That's quite a bit better than the 0.5% to 2% expense ratios for mutual funds (we'll discuss these in Chapter 6). In other words, we can categorize the SPY and DIA funds as low-cost funds.

In spite of low fees, the effectiveness of these index funds is remarkably high. In 2007, Warren Buffett made a $1 million dollar bet that over a ten-year term, the S&P 500 (SPY) index fund would outperform a collection of hedge funds selected by a manager of Protégé Partners, an asset management and advisory company based in New York. In 2017, Buffett won the bet: the index fund returned 7.1% compounded annually compared to 2.2% for the hedge funds selected by the manager. The real winner was a local girl's charity to which Buffett donated his winnings.

The results speak for themselves; I strongly recommend that you begin your investment career by buying one of these index funds. Afterwards, you can diversify your portfolio by incorporating the other strategies in this book.

The Bullet Points

- Inflation, which gradually decreases the value of currency, must be overcome in order for you to build wealth.

- Investing in stocks is a great way for you to accumulate wealth and offset the eroding value of money from inflation.

- By buying a stock, you become an owner of a share of the company.

- To buy and sell stocks, you must open an account at a brokerage.

- There are two types of brokerages: Discount Brokerages where the cost of trading is minimal and you're on your own; and Full-Service Brokerages where the cost of trading is higher, but you have a personal relationship with a broker.

- When buying and selling a stock, you can set your own price through a limit order.

- Most often, you will buy and sell stocks "at the market" which is the best price your brokerage can get for you.

- There are stock exchanges sprinkled throughout the world. I strongly recommend that you confine your buying of stocks to those listed on the New York Stock Exchange (NYSE) and NASDAQ Stock Exchange (NASDAQ).

- The actions of the Federal Reserve, which include monetary policy and the federal funds rate, influence the state of the U.S. economy and the market.

- The Dow Industrial Average fund (DIA) and the S&P 500 (SPY) mirrors the state of the market as a whole.

- You should monitor the performance of the companies in which you invest by reading the CEO's letter in the Annual Report.

- ETFs and Index Funds allow you to invest in stocks without placing all of your bets on the performance of a single company.

- Buy the S&P 500 and the DIA index funds! These should be the backbone of your portfolio.

2

THE MENTALITY OF THE SUCCESSFUL INVESTOR

The career of boxing's most iconic heavyweight champion began in an alleyway in Brooklyn, New York, when two young boys got into a dispute over a pigeon. The younger boy, who had domesticated a flock of the street birds, was incensed when the older bully purportedly ripped off the head of one of his favorite pets. The grisly act would not go unpunished; the younger boy fought his adversary and handily won. That was Mike Tyson's first knockout.

Seven years later, Tyson would become the youngest heavyweight champion in boxing history. His career reached stratospheric heights across the globe. "Iron Mike" evoked the shock and awe of anyone who watched him, not only for his dominance in the ring, but for his bizarre behavior outside of it. Over the course of his fighting career, Tyson accrued over $300 million. If handled correctly, that fortune would be enough to sustain a small country.

What Tyson had in a punishing right hook, he lacked in budgeting prowess. Upgrading from Brooklyn pigeons, he infamously kept full-grown Bengal tigers as pets. He had a fleet of luxury cars — Rolls Royces, Ferraris, Lamborghinis, and Jaguars, just to name a few — along with a number of sprawling mansions. When Tyson declared bankruptcy, he reminded us of a lesson that we should always remember: money isn't infinite.

This chapter will introduce you to ideas and concepts that allow you to succeed financially. Let's get started.

/

The Basic Rule of Investing: Risk & Reward

There was a time when the social success of human beings wasn't determined by how much money they made, but rather how much meat they had in their caves. Trading stocks may be a pretty new phenomenon in the timeline of human history, but the concepts that motivate investing behavior extend all the way back to prehistoric times.

Let's pretend that we're cave-people who have recently exhausted our stock of food. While we don't have any choice but to go out hunting, we can select what kind of animal we're going to chase. Are we gunning for smaller, less dangerous creatures like rabbits or birds? Or do we want to be more ambitious by going after a buffalo or a rhinoceros? Going after the smaller prey might be easier, but it won't provide much meat. On the other hand, killing a powerful beast could feed our tribe for weeks...the only issue is that it could kill us during the hunt.

Luckily, our lives aren't on the line when we invest in the modern day. But the same basic rule of investing applies:

As the potential for reward increases, the level of risk increases accordingly.

This rule should play a part in every investment decision that you make, from figuring out which type of investment is best for you to deciding on how much money you want to contribute to a given investment. Ultimately when you make an investment, you must accept the level of risk that accompanies it.

Because everyone interprets risk and reward differently, the basic rule of investing will lead to wildly different results across different investors. That being said, there are a few strong trends that work on a general scale.

Swing for the Fence When You're Young; Get on Base When You're Older

This rule is largely counter-intuitive, but it holds water when you really boil it down. If you're young and have decades of earning experience ahead of you, it makes sense to pursue riskier investments for several reasons. For starters, you have more earning years ahead of you when you're young. If a young person gets unlucky and an investment goes south, it's not the end of the world; your loss will probably be negligible in the big scheme of things. Young investors also have more time for a struggling stock to reverse its course and more time to make up losses with other investments.

Further, young investors should focus on growing their wealth whereas older investors should focus on sustaining their wealth. At the beginning of our career, we're chasing a quality of life that we're dreaming of. That could mean vastly different things to different people, but in order to accomplish our goals, we probably need to get richer. On the other hand, older investors have already settled into their lifestyles and typically don't have much need for growth. Risky investments don't make sense if you already have the things that you need.

The Importance of Budgeting: a Dollar Saved is Just as Valuable as a Dollar Earned

The authors Thomas Stanley and William Danko wrote a fascinating book titled *The Millionaire Next Door*, which aimed to determine the factors that have turned ordinary people into millionaires. The book lists seven common denominators among those who successfully build wealth. One of those factors — living modestly — applies to our conversation.

Living modestly is just as important to achieving financial success. Many people believe that building wealth is about making money, but that's only one side of the token. In reality, building wealth is about making more money than you spend. There are tons of people who have astronomical incomes but still manage to live beyond their means. Don't let that be you!

It doesn't matter how much money you earn; if you don't have a framework that allows you to save and invest, you won't be able to sustain your financial goals. Having a poor budgeting plan is like having a leaky boat. No matter how well you can bail out the water, the ocean will keep creeping in.

Have you ever noticed that the world's richest people have a tendency to be modest with their finances? Warren Buffet, whose net worth has been approximated at $79.2 billion, is still living in the house he bought in 1958 for $31,500. He claims to refuse spending over $4 dollars on breakfast. A breakfast tab may seem like drops in the bucket to someone like Buffet, but it's his mentality towards the dollar that has made him so wealthy. Every penny saved is a penny earned. I'm not advocating for you to pinch pennies; I'm encouraging you to be aware of what you spend. Especially in today's age where our credit cards are synced to our smartphones, it's easier than ever to spend. But before you give you money away, ask yourself if you really want what you're buying. Is it filling a need in your life, or is it going to make you significantly happier? If so, swipe away your credit card. But if not, contribute that would-be expense to an investment fund.

To develop sound budgeting habits, I recommend keeping a detailed record of your monthly earnings and your monthly expenses. By comparing these two figures at the end of each month, you'll be able to see how well you're saving. If you aren't saving money each month, you won't have any ammunition for your investment accounts.

I would add one more factor to Stanley and Danko's study: avoid debt at all costs. The only exception to my debt rule is when the time comes to buy a house; then, you'll need to take out a mortgage. Having debt means having to pay interest, which can suffocate one's finances. One of the worst things you can do is fall into the trap of credit card debt. While it might not seem like you're spending money every time that you swipe a credit card, it isn't free money. Falling behind on credit card payments will subject you to penalty fees and interest payments that eat away at your income. Debt can sap the funds that you should use for investing, and investing is where your future wealth lies.

The Big Secret: Becoming a Long-Term Investor

In 1953, the British writer Ian Fleming sat down at his desk to write his very first spy novel. As he went scrawling away at the first draft of *Casino Royale,* he never expected that he was crafting one of the most iconic fictional characters of our time: James Bond. Interestingly enough, Fleming had no intentions of doing this. In a 1962 interview published in *The New Yorker,* he stated, "I wanted Bond to be an extremely dull, uninteresting man to whom things happened; I wanted him to be a blunt instrument. [...] When I was casting around for a name for my protagonist, I thought my God, James Bond is the dullest name I ever heard."

The figure of James Bond has assumed a mythic status in our culture, synonymous with class, masculinity, and power. But if we peel back the layers, Bond certainly has his problems. He isn't particularly deep or caring, often indulging in whiskey, cigarettes, and sexual exploits. He doesn't have a compelling backstory or any motivation for saving the world on endless occasions. And he doesn't have a clear character arc throughout the novels. In short, James Bond isn't much more than a handsome killing machine with an endless supply of suggestive one-liners. All of this begs the question...why do we love James Bond?

I'm not a literary critic, but I believe our culture loves James Bond for his sense of composure amidst chaos. Whether he's facing a nuclear threat or a high-beamed laser inching towards him, Bond is unfazed by the circumstances that surround him. We never see him act brashly, and we never see him panic. He has the confidence that no matter how bad things seem in the present moment, everything will turn out okay.

This exact mentality is how we need to act as investors. Rather than panicking and being swayed by short-term swings in the market, we need to retain our cool and have faith that the market will continue its upward trend. This isn't always easy. When I saw my stock portfolio take a dive in the 2007 recession, all I wanted to do was liquidate my investments before they dropped any lower. Instead, I watched

Goldeneye and let the market run its course. All of those stocks bounced back over the next few years. Just like James Bond, I skirted disaster by keeping calm.

What exactly is long-term investing?

Long-term investing is a strategy that minimizes the risks of the stock market by relying on the upward trend of the market. Rather than buying and selling stocks for quick gains or losses, long-term investing is all about sitting on an investment for years at a time. Ultimately, what I'm suggesting is remarkably simple: do your research into a stock, and once the transaction is made... be patient. Can you think of another context in which doing nothing yields the most reward? Pretty convenient for us novices who have busy lives.

If you fancy data over assurances, take a look at the following table. This lists the closing price of the DJIA on the last trading day of each year, for the past 50 years at 5-year intervals.

Year	Dow Jones Industrial Average (DJIA)
1973	850
1978	805
1983	1,258
1988	2,168
1993	3,154
1998	9,181
2003	10,453
2008	8,776
2013	16,576
2018	23,327

Decimals not included on DJIA data
Data from MarketWatch's Historical Stock Quotes

As you can see, the stock market has gone up, sometimes dramatically. While stock market declines may occur from time-to-time, the market is undefeated in the long-run.

Jeremy Siegel, the respected Professor of Finance at the Wharton School at the University of Pennsylvania, conducted a study into the effectiveness of long-term investing. From 1802 to 1992, Professor Siegel compared the total returns on four assets: gold, short-term bonds, long-term bonds, and stocks. The data showed that stocks outperformed the other investments by a healthy margin. Despite the exception of the Great Depression (from which the country ultimately recovered), the stock market has had an ongoing upward projection.

If we know that we're supposed to embrace long-term investments, the question becomes how long is long-term? Of course the answer varies with respect to the stock; I recommend holding a stock until you have a clear reason to sell. That could be attributable to a change in the industry, reorganization of leadership, or an emerging competitor. Whatever it may be, you should hold a stock until there's a tangible, definite reason for selling.

When asked how long an investor should hold a stock, the inimitable Warren Buffet had a two-word answer: "probably forever." This is probably impractical for investors like you and me who want to enjoy our profits one day. But if our goal was to maximize the value of our portfolio, the correct strategy would be to never take our money out of the market.

John Maynard Keynes, the founder of the Keynesian Theory of Economics, was famous for coining the axiom: "The market can remain irrational longer than you can remain solvent." In other words, the market doesn't have emotions, and it doesn't care what we think. The market is like the weather in Boston; just because it's doing something in one moment doesn't mean we can predict what it will do in the next. All of this to say — who knows what's going to happen! All we can do is trust that the market will prevail over time.

The flip side: frequent trading

On the other side of the fence from long-term investors, there are frequent traders who try to outsmart the market by making quick transactions. But even worse than frequent trading is day trading, the strategy of buying a stock in the morning and selling later the same day. If you decide to become a day trader after reading this book, I will have failed miserably; it's a sure way to the poor house. Here's why: while we know that the market will rise over time, it's impossible to know what it will do in the short-term. In other words, we can't time the market. The most successful capitalists in American history would agree with this statement. When J. P. Morgan, founder and head of the Morgan Bank, was asked by John D. Rockefeller, the head of Standard Oil, what the price of Standard Oil's stock will be, Morgan's answer was simple. "It will fluctuate." In other words, the price was impossible to predict in the short-term.

If you think about it, frequent trading doesn't make any sense. First of all, brokerage fees and commissions are an ongoing expense for the frequent trader, significantly lessening the profits and accentuating the losses on investments. But more importantly, stocks aren't seasonal; their prices don't fluctuate on a predictable basis. Take the tariff dispute between the United States and China that occurred during 2018 and early 2019. This international event rippled throughout our economy, causing quick drops in growth stocks. Unless you have an in with our country's foreign policy department, there's no way that you would be able to predict that the dispute would occur. And even if you did have that insight, you wouldn't be able to act on it — that would be insider trading. So if fluctuation is a function of information — not trends — the argument for frequent trading loses all of its wind. Rather, we should disregard variations in the stock market and commit to our investments until we have reason to change our perspective.

Avoid the Herd Effect

The most common error that people make is getting influenced by the herd effect; that is, purchasing a stock because friends or colleagues are buying it. You might think your friends are smart and savvy, but who's to say that they've done their homework? One form of the herd effect is called momentum investing, in which a person buys a stock because the price is going up. This is another critical error — remember that no one can predict what a stock is going to do in the short term. Just because it's rising today doesn't mean it will continue to rise tomorrow. Ultimately, the only way to feel comfortable about a stock is to conduct your own research before purchasing.

In Warren Buffet's introduction to Benjamin Graham's book *The Intelligent Investor,* he lays out what he deems the most important trait for successful investing:

> "To invest successfully over a lifetime does not require a stratospheric IQ, unusual business insights, or inside information. What's needed is a strong intellectual framework for making decisions, and the ability to keep emotions from corroding that framework."

To put it another way, don't let the whims and comments of others become the sole motivation for an investment. You should consider what others have to say, especially if you value their opinions, but making an investment should ultimately come down to your decision-making abilities.

The Importance of Being Observant

When we're investing, what are we really doing? We aren't contributing to a company's operations, nor are we generating sales or performing services. Rather, we're selecting a company that we think will succeed in the marketplace.

Let's think of this in terms of a horse race. The CEO is the trainer, the employees are the jockey, and the thoroughbred is the company's performance. What role do we play as investors? Well, we're the bettors watching in the grandstands. We aren't involved in the horse's training regimen or its workout, nor do we have to get in the saddle and maneuver the horse to victory. Instead, our job is to observe. We're responsible for looking at all the variables of the race:

- Which horses are racing?
- How old are they, and what are their racing records?
- What are the bloodlines of each horse, and how successful have their siblings been?
- Is the track made of turf or dirt?

We even have the luxury of walking down to the paddock and watching the horses before they trot off towards the starting gate. This can bring up a new flock of questions, aside from the ones that have cropped up from our research:

- Are any of the horses wearing leg wraps? If so, could they be nursing an injury?
- Which horses look tired? Which ones look energized?
- Does one horse look particularly more athletic than the others?

All in all, it's our job to collect data that can allow us to predict who will win the race. We don't have any impact on the outcome; we simply have the freedom to select a horse. As investors, our success is determined by how well we notice things. That extends not only to details about a company like its leadership structure, financials, and marketing campaigns, but to certain sectors of the economy. For example, perhaps you're noticing a significant uptick of electric cars on your morning commute...what does that say about the oil business? Should we expect fossil fuels to take a dive over the next few decades? Ultimately, we should treat every current event as valuable data that can inform our investment decisions.

The Fallacy of Heroics

Our culture loves to celebrate heroes. Time and time again, we line up at the theaters to watch Superman swat down a bevy of bullets. We tune into ESPN to watch Serena Williams scorch her opponents on a serve, or Lebron James dunk on his opponents. But financial success scarcely works this way. In the world of business and investing, success isn't determined by a heroic act; it's determined by doing all the small things in the right sequence.

Take two friends graduating from college at the same time. Let's say that they pursued the same degree, earned the same grades, and have the same level of intelligence. Both of them decide to start small businesses in the same industry — call it fitness. The only difference between these friends is that the first one is affected by hero culture while the second friend focuses on the small things. The first friend tries to hook a marlin straight off the bat — he spends his time trying to recruit figures like Dwayne "The Rock" Johnson and Arnold Schwarzenegger to pump iron at his gym. The second friend, however, does all the little things in the right order. He develops a functional website, begins a cost-effective marketing campaign, and voices promotions to the community. Unless the first friend gets lucky, his business probably won't take off while the second friend will probably have success.

This is a good thing for us — it means that growing wealth is something that we can all do if we remain organized and disciplined.

The 3 Approaches to Investing

We've already established that common stocks are a great option for the novice investor. With that in mind, I want to walk you through the three strategies that you can use in your investment career.

Approach 1: Hire a Professional

If you're an investor who doesn't have the time, inclination, or patience to do your own investing, hire a professional. Before hiring someone, I suggest researching potential candidates. The following metrics are most important:

- What's the professional's investing strategy? Do they gravitate towards long-term or short-term investing?
- What types of stocks does the professional gravitate toward? What types of industries have they bought into?
- What types of investments does the professional favor? Common stocks, mutual funds, fixed securities (bonds, treasuries, etc)?
- What's the professional's track record over the past several years?
- What fees does the professional charge?

A deeper dive into fees, as these are critical. Fee structures can vary across the board, but as a novice investor, you should seek someone who charges a flat fee. Another good idea is to upgrade from a discount brokerage to a full-service brokerage; by doing this, your broker will act as your adviser and your fee will be the brokerage's commissions on every transaction.

Once your portfolio reaches a certain value, you'll want to work with more seasoned professionals who charge an annual percent of your portfolio's total assets. While this percent varies and is often negotiable, standard guidelines are noted below:

- 1%: For portfolios with assets under $1 million
- ½%: For portfolios with assets over $1 million

Approach 2: Buy a Stable Index Fund

If you want to avoid the fees charged by a professional investor but don't want to select individual stocks, I suggest strategy 2: buy shares of an index fund. The best ones are the S&P 500 (SPY) or the Dow Jones Industrial Fund (DIA). As discussed at the end of Chapter 1, owning shares of an index fund is one of the best and easiest ways to invest in the stock market.

Approach 3: Select your Own Stocks and Exchange Traded Funds

Many investors want the challenge of selecting individual stocks. If you want to take this path, I applaud your ambition! However, you must recognize that you're competing against thousands of people. Many of these are professionals with advanced degrees in finance who spend all day analyzing the stock market with sophisticated computer programs. Succeeding against the pros is possible, but it requires diligence and commitment. If you subscribe to this strategy, make sure that you stick to long-term investing and pick stocks that rely on the innovation and growth of the United States economy.

If you're interested in pursuing this third strategy, I've devoted the next chapter to laying out different strategies for discovering worthwhile stocks. Finding companies that are worthy of your investment dollars is the biggest challenge for any self-guided investor, but it's exciting and doable.

/

Stealing from the Pros: Investment Strategies from the Kings of Wall Street

I've given you some of my thoughts on investing strategies, but there are many more that may appeal to you. Here's a selection of perspectives, all published by authorities in the finance world, which you may find interesting for your portfolio. Each of these strategies have served me well at one time or another during my investment career.

Buy what you know (Peter Lynch)

Peter Lynch, the former head of the Magellan Fund, encourages people to invest in companies with which they're familiar. You may come to 'know' a company through your professional experience or by being a consumer of that business' products or services. As an example, if you're a physician, you probably know a lot about new drugs and the pharmaceutical companies. If you work in real estate, you probably have expertise in housing and building materials.

Bet on the tortoise, not the hare (Howard Marks)

Howard Marks, co-founder and chairman of Oaktree Capital Management, published a strategy arguing that "consistency trumps drama." In other words, don't bite on the companies with dramatic spikes, as they're rarely sustainable. Rather, you should make your investments based on the actual value of a company. As we've discussed, it's impossible to give a definitive assessment of value, but it's a good start to look at consistency over a period of many years. This strategy shares some DNA with my thoughts on the fallacy of heroics. Instead of focusing on the home run stock, we should chase reliable investments in the marketplace.

Be the fish that swims against the stream (John Templeton)

John Templeton, founder of the Templeton fund, became successful by being a contrarian. Templeton searched for depressed stocks that had fallen out of favor with the market. For example, if everyone seems to be hyped on oil companies, Templeton might suggest investing in the electric car industry. The idea makes sense — when the market has doubts about a company, prices will drop and present a lucrative investing opportunity.

Another way of understanding Templeton's philosophy is by thinking about optimism and pessimism. When the market is optimistic about a certain company or industry, it's time to be cautious. Conversely, pessimistic feelings indicate that it's time to buy. Warren Buffet expressed the same idea in different words: "Be fearful when everyone is greedy, and be greedy when everyone is fearful."

Templeton's approach requires guts! Think about it — in order for a company to be worthy of your investment, it must be outside of public favor. If your portfolio follows Templeton's guidelines, it's inclined to be questioned by the general public. That being said, the ideas that support Templeton's ideas are sound.

Efficient Market Theory / The Rational Market

Because public information about a company's business is available to all investors, many consider the current stock price to be a fair price. This is called "The Efficient Market Theory," or "The Rational Market." The premise of Efficient Market Theory may sound obvious, but it leads to an interesting conclusion. If the price of a stock at any given moment is fair, investors shouldn't be focused on projecting whether a given stock is over or undervalued. In other words, proponents of Efficient Market Theory don't buy stocks because a price is low enough to meet their standards. Rather, they make their buying decisions based on the likelihood that the company will grow and become more valuable.

Though the Efficient Market Theory has been challenged by some economists, I find this strategy helpful. Rather than trying to 'get a steal' on a stock, it's much better to simply assess whether a company is likely to become more successful over time. We'll discuss this in Chapter 4, but one of my biggest investing mistakes was waiting for a stock's price to drop to an arbitrary level that had no real basis. I believed in the company, but I was too hung up on pricing and ultimately passed on an investment that would have turned a strong profit.

Strategies to be Wary of

Now that we've covered the investment strategies that I have found useful, I want to introduce you to a few popular philosophies that contrast with my way of thinking. I don't suggest following these strategies, but you're bound to encounter them throughout your career and it may be useful to know what they entail.

The Dogs of the Dow

The Dogs of the Dow is an often-quoted investment strategy based on buying stocks on the first trading day of the year. Here's how it works: out of the 30 companies that make up the Dow Jones Industrial Average, the investor selects the 10 companies with the highest dividend yield (we'll discuss dividends and yield in Chapter 3). In the following year, the investor rebalances his or her portfolio to include the current top-ten companies for dividend yield. The strategy is based on the idea that the ten companies with the highest yield would have had the worst year, and their stock should theoretically rebound in the coming year. The results over the past 20 years have shown that the Dogs of the Dow strategy led to roughly the same results as an investor who bought and held all 30 stocks that comprise the DJIA. In other words, it was a whole lot of hassle for not much return.

The Small Dogs of the Dow is the exact same strategy, except instead of buying 10 stocks, the investor buys the 5 highest-yielding stocks on the DJIA. While the results have historically been slightly better for the Small Dogs of the Dow strategy, they aren't all that significant. The analysis also didn't take into account the fees from all of that buying and selling — remember that you have to pay a brokerage commission on each of your transactions.

The Dogs of the Dow strategy is not recommended for the individual investor: it goes against my philosophy of being a long-term investor.

Greenblatt's Magic Formula (Joel Greenblatt)

A "Magic Formula" for selecting stocks was developed by Joel Greenblatt, founder and managing partner of Graham Capital. Greenblatt develops and explains the formula over the course of his book *The Little Book That Beats the Market*. Basically, the formula recommends buying approximately 30 stocks of the largest companies that have the highest return on capital and the highest earnings yield. While Greenblatt shows how he determines these values in his book, an approximation for Return on Capital is Return on Equity (ROE); and an approximation for Earnings Yield is Price Earnings Ratio (P/E). I bring this up because I'll teach you how to find and analyze ROE and P/E in the next chapter.

Greenblatt says that by using his formula over the prior 17 years, a portfolio would have returned approximately 30% per year compared to a return of approximately 12% per year for the overall market. Greenblatt adds the caveat that a portfolio using his formula would have failed to beat the market once every four years. To compensate for the down years, one must stay with the formula long-term to be successful. My criticism of Greenblatt's "Magic Formula" is the same as my criticism of the Dogs of the Dow; it is the opposite of long-term investing because the formula requires the investor to rebalance his or her portfolio every year.

Look at the calendar (Hirsch and Mistal)

Jeffrey Hirsch and Christopher Mistal, two authors of the Stock Trader's Almanac, chart market behavior based on the calendar. Hirsch and Mistal believe that aspects like days of the month, months of the year, seasonal variations, presidential elections, and holidays have a significant and predictable effect on the market. Two of their well-known indices are the "January Effect" and "So Goes January, So Goes The Market." They found that stocks are often sold in December, likely for tax purposes, and then bought in January. Further, they found that there's a 75% probability that if the market is up at the end of January, it will be up at the end of the year. The converse is true: if January is a down month, it's likely to be a down year for the market. Such information might appeal to short-term investors, but it has little relevance for those holding stocks for the long-term.

/

The Bullet Points

- A greater opportunity for reward means a greater level of risk. You must accept the risk that accompanies every investment that you make.

- Select one (or more) of the 3 investing methods (hiring a professional, buying a stable index fund, selecting your own stocks).

- Budgeting skills are just as important as investing prowess.

- Success isn't accomplished by big, flashy moves; it's accomplished by doing the small things in the right sequence.

- Every great investor is a great observer of the commercial world.

- Be a long-term investor and avoid frequent trading like the plague!

3

HOW TO CHOOSE A COMMON STOCK

In my career as a surgeon, I kept accurate records of the operations I performed. Those records ended up providing valuable insight into which procedures were best for certain conditions. I wanted to share my findings with colleagues; however, before my work could be accepted for publication, I needed to show that my results were valid. In other words, I required the help of a statistician. Luckily, I found the perfect person to help me: a statistics instructor at the Cedars-Sinai Medical Center in Los Angeles. With her assistance, my findings were published. Unfortunately, she wouldn't remain available for long.

"Dr. Treiman," she told me one day, "I won't be able to help you with any more of your research projects."

"Why is that?"

"I got a job at a company called Amgen."

I'd never heard of this company, which has since become a leader in American pharmaceuticals. At first she agreed to help me in her spare time, but after a while she got so busy that she had no time for me.

"If a woman that smart is that busy," I thought to myself, "Amgen must be a pretty good company." I ended up buying 300 shares of Amgen stock, each of which were selling for about $47.13 As of 2019, the price per share has ballooned to over $240. I still hold that stock today.

My Amgen investment mirrored Peter Lynch's philosophy of buying what you know. But over the years, I came to buy stocks by looking at a number of metrics that helped me determine good stocks from bad stocks. This chapter will introduce you to these concepts so that you can effectively appraise a stock for potential investment.

/

Finding Stocks: The 2 Approaches

In general, there are two ways to find companies: the top-down approach, and the bottom-up approach. While these two approaches are not exclusionary and complement each other nicely, it's useful to distinguish between the two. Let's dive into both…

The Top-Down Approach

The Top-Down approach involves identifying sectors in the economy that are ripe for growth. Once you figure out which industries are expanding, you can select companies that are innovating those industries. In making investment decisions, try to understand which industries are developing new and exciting products; and within those industries, companies that have the best product and whose stock is selling at a fair price.

The top-down investor may be inclined to invest in exchange traded funds (ETFs), as these investment opportunities group companies by industry. If you feel confident about which sectors of the economy are growing, selecting suitable ETFs and using the top-down approach can be a winning strategy.

The Bottom-Up Approach

The bottom-up approach is the inverse of the top-down approach. Rather than starting with a sector of the economy, the investor scouts for individual companies that look like they'll do well for a long time. If that stock succeeds over time, the investor may invest in other companies within the same industry.

You can see that each of these approaches can produce the same result. As you search for companies to invest in, I encourage you to try each approach. You'll soon find that you're inclined to one over the other.

Buy American

When buying individual stocks, you should limit your search to companies headquartered in the United States. This is because the rules for reporting businesses are held to a constant standard in the states. While a massively profitable company based in Europe or Asia may seem like a great opportunity, there are numerous tax and reporting laws that make these investments simply too complicated for our sake.

Also, buying companies in countries that speak foreign languages make it nearly impossible to stay on top of corporate activity. You never want to be in a position in which you don't understand the happenings of the businesses that you've invested in. Rest assured there isn't a shortage of companies to choose from in the United States.

The Nitty-Gritty: How to appraise the value of a stock for purchase

Any man who's fallen in love with the woman he wants to marry will soon face the terrifying puzzle of selecting the right diamond. These poor romantics are fated to navigating "The Four Cs": color, clarity, cut, and carat. Of course, there are countless other decisions to manage once the diamond is selected. What color will the band be? How should the prongs be designed? What size is the girlfriend's ring finger?

These tasks seem all but impossible for someone with zero background in jewelry. The same goes for selecting a stock for purchase. If you're facing these concepts for the first time, don't be discouraged if they seem confusing at first. Once you understand the vocabulary and the acronyms, everything will come into focus.

Stocks are difficult to appraise, largely because their prices are always fluctuating in the market. The goal of this section is to give you the tools to determine which stocks are most likely to increase in value and are fairly priced. You can also use this section to evaluate a stock that you're considering selling. However, I say that through gritted teeth — you should stick to your guns of long-term investing.

Checking under the hood: where do I find the details about a given stock?

In order for us to appraise a stock, we need a source that lays out the details and information of that company. While there are tons of resources on the internet, I use the following website:

www.finance.yahoo.com

Here, you can enter the name or symbol of the company that you want to appraise, and the subheadings will show information on all of the material that I'm about to discuss. When the stock market is open, you may notice this information changing in real-time — that's because the data is based on the last trade of a live market. When the stock market is closed, the information on this website will show data based on the last trade that was made before closing.

Categorizing Stocks: Large Cap, Small Cap, Value, and Growth

Stocks are categorized as large cap and small cap, and between value and growth. A large cap stock has a market value over $1 billion, whereas a small cap stock has a market value under $1 billion. Cap is an abbreviation for capitalization and can be found by multiplying the total number of shares available by the price per share. Think of large cap stocks as a steamship moving slowly and steadily across the ocean. Small cap stocks are like a speedboat that can move more quickly but are always vulnerable to being overturned by a big wave.

Large cap stocks are safer for the beginning investor because they're less volatile and easier to sell. That being said, small cap stocks tend to outperform large cap stocks over long periods of time. None of this should come as a surprise, especially in light of the basic rule of investing: more risk comes with a greater chance of reward. Successful large cap stocks are easier to find because they get lots of attention. Apple, Amazon, and Google are a few of the major large caps in today's market.

We can also organize stocks by classifying them as value or growth. Value stocks tend to be stable, risk-averse, and well-settled in their industries. While there are exceptions, many value stocks are also large cap stocks. Value stocks also tend to pay dividends, which we'll get to later in the chapter. On the other side of the spectrum, growth stocks are investments that are expected to outpace the market over the next several years. They may not be worth as much as a value stock in the present, but they tend to have more upside and more risk. Growth stocks pay little or no dividends to shareholders, as every cent of profit goes towards growing the business. You can clearly distinguish between value stocks and growth stocks by looking at a metric called the P/E ratio (we'll discuss this below). Companies with P/Es close to the historic average of '15' are considered value stocks, whereas companies with higher P/Es are considered growth stocks.

Ideally, your portfolio should incorporate a mix of large and small caps, and value and growth stocks. Doing so will diversify your portfolio, with small caps and growth stocks giving you plenty of room for future profit, and large caps and value stocks preventing you from burdening yourself with too much risk.

Price per Share

Price per Share is exactly what it sounds like: the cost of each share of stock. As you'd expect, you're searching for stocks that have a low price per share, at least in relation to what you think it will be in the future. Price per Share is used to determine the value of your present holdings.

52-Week High and Low

This figure consists of two numbers: the highest and lowest price per share of a given stock over the past year. The 52-week high and low is a good way to measure the consistency of a stock. Less risky stocks have a relatively small difference between the high and low, while more volatile stocks are evidenced by big gaps. If you notice polar numbers in the 52-week high and low, I suggest determining the cause before buying.

Beta Value

While we can't eliminate risk, we can minimize the threat that it poses to us by monitoring it carefully. The best metric for quantifying risk is "beta," which measures the volatility of a stock in comparison to the market. A beta of '1' means that the stock trades in tandem with the market; we can interpret this to be a neutral risk rating. When beta is greater than '1,' the stock is more volatile than the market — that is, the stock price will have higher highs and lower lows in relation to the collective market. Betas that are less than '1' reflect less volatile stocks.

Book Value & Price/Book

Book Value is a measurement of how much a company is actually worth. It's determined by subtracting a company's liabilities from the total assets. What's important to you as the investor is the Price/Book. This is an indication of how much Book Value you receive for buying a share of stock. You can find this figure on any financial website.

We can interpret the Price/Book by classifying the result as either less or more than '1.' Ultimately, you're looking for the lowest Price/Book figures that you can find. When Price/Book is less than '1', the Price per Share is lower than the Book Value per Share (BVPS); in other words, you're paying a smaller amount than you'd receive if the company went belly-up. On the other hand, a number greater than '1' indicates that you're paying a premium for the stock. Evaluating Price/Book is a great way to appraise a stock, but it's important to appreciate that this is just one criterion amidst a sea of data. Many great stocks are running with Price/Books greater than '1.'

Price/Earning Ratio (P/E)

Price/Earning Ratio (P/E) is the relationship between how much money the company is making and the Price Per Share. This is one of the most widely used criteria for determining if a stock is fairly priced. The P/E is obtained by dividing the Price Per Share by the Earnings Per Share (EPS). We've already discussed Price Per Share at length; Earnings Per Share is a figure calculated by dividing the total amount that a company makes by the shares outstanding. See below for an example:

Price Per Share: $100
Earnings Per Share (EPS): $5
100 / 5 = **20**

Now let's say that EPS doubles to $10...

Price/Share: $100
Earnings/Share (EPS): $10
100 / 10 = **10**

As you can see, higher earnings drive the P/E down. That means that you're generally searching for companies with relatively low P/Es. The lower the P/E, the less risk there is to the stock price if the company doesn't meet future expectations. On the contrary, high P/Es indicate that the stock price will plummet if the company underperforms. Although P/Es for individual companies vary, the average P/E for the market has historically been around 15. That essentially means that the stock is selling at 15 times its current earnings. Another way to look at this metric is to understand that the P/E value is the number of years it would take for the company to earn the cost of a share at present earnings. The reason that people buy shares at a P/E greater than '1' relates to the expectation that earnings will increase over time.

Now, this isn't to say that you should only buy companies with low P/Es. Many valuable stocks have sky-high PEs; in fact at the time of this writing, Amazon has a P/E of ~76! That doesn't mean that it's a bad investment; it just means that the company's earnings aren't high enough to substantially offset the stock price. Investing in a company with a high P/E doesn't mean that you've chosen a bad company; it just means that you're paying a premium for that stock.

Dividends and Yield

The primary value from stocks will always come from the appreciation of price per share over time. But some companies offer a second avenue for profit through something called dividends. Dividends are payments that a company distributes to its stockholders from the profits of that company, and they serve as an added incentive to purchase shares. Think of a dividend like whipped cream on top of a dessert: it's not the reason you order the item, but it adds to the enjoyment. As you build a portfolio, I recommend scouting for a few high yield stocks that promise income through dividends.

Now, not all companies pay dividends; some prefer to use the cash from their profits to further the business. Two very good companies that do not pay dividends are Amazon (AMZN) and Berkshire Hathaway (BRK-A or BRK-B — these correspond to two classes of Berkshire Hathaway, one of which sells for a fraction of the other). In general, value stocks pay dividends, whereas growth stocks tend to pump their extra cash back into the business.

Right now, I'm talking about dividends from common stocks — not from preferred stocks, which have different rules that we'll discuss later. For common stocks, the company's management decides the amount of the dividend and how often the dividend will be paid. Bear in mind — and this is particularly important if you're buying a stock for its dividend — management has the authority to continue, increase, decrease, or stop the dividend entirely! During the financial crisis in 2007, many companies that previously paid a dividend stopped doing so in order to conserve cash. If you're buying a stock primarily for its dividend, you should check the company's dividend history. There are companies that have paid a dividend every year for many years, and there are companies that have increased their dividends every year for over 10 years. Lists of these 5-star dividend payers can be found through a quick internet search.

As noted, management decides on the amount of the dividend for the coming year and how it will be paid; however, most dividends are paid four times a year. Despite these quarterly payments, the amount of a dividend is quoted as a yearly or annual disbursement. If you're buying a stock for its dividend or selling a stock that pays a dividend, there are two important dates to know: the record date and the ex-dividend date. The record date is when you must be listed as a stockholder to be eligible to receive the dividend. The ex-dividend date, usually one business day prior to the record date, is the date on which the shares are traded without the dividend. How do these dates play out in real life? If you want to buy a stock that pays a good dividend, buy it before the ex-dividend date in order to receive the dividend. If you want to sell a stock without losing the dividend, sell it after the record date.

Instead of paying a cash dividend, some companies will issue stock dividends, or dividends as shares of stock. Companies use stock dividends to preserve cash while maintaining a dividend. If you're wondering where these reserve shares come from, every company preserves shares of their own stock that they can use to buy other companies, compensate executives, or issue dividends to their shareholders. Unlike regular dividends, which you must report as income to the IRS every year, stock dividends are not subject to tax until the stock is sold.

A stock dividend is usually a fraction of an additional share for every share owned. For example, a 10% annual stock dividend would mean that for every ten shares owned, you receive one share of stock. It isn't a problem if your number of shares comes out as a fraction, as companies keep track of fractional shares and will properly value your investment.

Now, because additional shares dilute the total number of shares available to be traded, the stock price for companies that administer stock dividends tends to drop by roughly the same percent as the stock dividend. That is, if a company pays a 10% stock dividend, the going stock price will probably drop by about 10%.

What's important for the stockholder is not the amount of the cash dividend, but how it compares to the price of the stock. This figure is called dividend yield. In general, higher yielding stocks are more attractive to value investors. But don't forget: yield is never set in stone. Because stock prices can change daily and the amount of the dividend can change quarterly, you should always keep an eye on yield, especially if a high yield was your motivation for purchasing a stock.

We can calculate the yield, which is always noted as a percent, by dividing the annual dividend by the price of the stock and then multiplying the resulting fraction by '100' to convert to a percent. Take a look below:

Company A

- Price per share: $50
- Annual dividend: $2

$$2 / 50 = 0.04$$
$$.04 \times 100 = \textbf{4\% yield}$$

Company B

- Price per share: $100
- Annual dividend: $2

$$2 / 100 = 0.02$$
$$.02 \times 100 = \textbf{2\% yield}$$

Note that while each of these companies are paying the same dividend, their yields are different because of the difference in the price of their stocks. I mention this formula to give you an understanding of what yield is, but you can find yield on the financial website of your choice.

If you're buying a stock for yield, what's the threshold above which you should consider making the transaction? In other words, how can you determine what a good yield really is? We can arrive at a solid answer by looking at the Consumer Price Index (CPI). The CPI, which we discussed earlier, mirrors the inflation rate and presently hovers just over 2%. This benchmark indicates that a 'good' yield is over 3% and preferably 4%. Anything less, and you're swimming against the tides of inflation.

A final note on dividends: they're subject to being heavily taxed, which is an annoyance that no one can avoid. Before administering the dividend, the company is taxed at a corporate rate. Only after the company subtracts this corporate tax from gross profits can the company administer dividends to its shareholders. But Uncle Sam isn't satisfied yet; before the dividend goes into your bank account, you have to pay tax on the dividend again! In other words, your dividend is taxed twice: first by the company; and second, by you. There isn't anything that you can do about this, but it's worth knowing as you consider how much of your investment strategy should rely on dividends.

Return on Equity (ROE)

Return on equity (ROE), is a percentage that represents how profitable a company is in relation to its equity. You've probably heard the term equity thrown around before; it can be understood as the total assets of a company minus its liabilities, or the net assets of a company. In simple terms, ROE measures how well a company has used the money invested by stockholders to increase its profits. Sanford Sigoloff, an expert in evaluating and turning around distressed companies, said that ROE was the single most important criterion in finding a well-run company. Sigoloff advises the investor to seek companies with an ROE of 15% or higher.

You can calculate ROE by dividing a company's annual net income by the average shareholder equity. Don't be thrown by the formula; you can find it under 'Management Effectiveness' on the financial website of your choice.

Financial Reports (Balance Sheet, Income Statement, Cash Flow)

Every publicly-traded company issues reports to its stockholders on how the company is doing. These 'financial reports' are jam-packed with dense information designed for the trained investor. Luckily, much of this information isn't necessary for achieving success in the stock market. The important parts for us novices are the balance sheet, income statement, and cash flow.

Financial reports are submitted to stockholders quarterly and annually and made available to the public on a regular basis. You can find these reports through a simple Google search. While quarterly reports break up a company's data into three-month periods for the past year, annual reports reflect a company's yearly performance over the past five years.

When reviewing quarterly financials, remember that business fluctuates throughout the course of a year. For example, if you own shares of the Hasbro toy company, the January, February, and March report may show higher profits than other quarters because the company would be reporting results from the holiday season. For that reason, I find annual financials far more useful than quarterly ones. By reviewing yearly financial statements, you can get a sense of how a company is doing and gain insight into its future direction. The investor should accept that some financial reports may be less impressive than others. I suggest adhering to the principles of long-term investing and avoid selling stocks after reading a disappointing financial report. However, if the disappointing results persist, it's time to perk up your ears and look at the company in depth. In the next chapter, when we discuss my best and worst investments, I'll tell you about the mistakes that I made by disregarding worrisome financial reports.

Before we dive into a breakdown on the balance sheet, income statement, and cash flow, let me shed light on a few of the most common acronyms that litter financials:

- **YOY** — year over year
- **TTM** — trailing twelve months. This means that a figure isn't making future projects; rather, it's looking back on what the company has done over the past year.
- **MRQ** — most recent quarter

Also, note that most numbers are reported in thousands. Just add three zeros to the number being referenced to find the actual dollar amount. The exception to this rule are values given per share of stock, such as Net Asset Value per Share (NAV/Share) or Earnings per Share (EPS).

The Balance Sheet lists a company's Assets and Liabilities. Assets include everything that the company owns such as cash, inventory, receivables, and property. Liabilities are the opposite of assets; they include everything that the company owes such as loans and other financial obligations. It follows that you can find what a company is worth by subtracting Liabilities from Assets. This figure is known as the Net Asset Value.

If you're reading carefully, the Net Asset Value should ring a bell. We've already covered a metric that subtracts Assets from Liabilities: Price/Book. NAV and Book Value are admittedly very similar, and novice investors like you and me shouldn't get too hung up on the difference. But if you're interested, Book Value excludes preferred shares of stock, which we'll cover in Chapter 6. It's also commonly used in the context of companies as opposed to funds. I mention NAV separately from Book/Value because it's found in the Balance Sheet.

There's one trick that companies use to inflate their Net Asset Value, and it involves something called Good Will. We can understand Good Will to be what a company considers their name to be worth. Take Apple as an example — even if Android releases a new phone with a far superior camera than the iPhone, the Apple brand is strong enough to prevent many buyers from trading in their devices. The problem with calculating Good Will is that it's subjective. While it's impossible to put a conclusive value on Good Will, the Balance Sheet tries by recording it as an Intangible Asset — that is, something of value that can't be physically held. By inflating Good Will (reported as Intangible Assets), companies can increase the Net Asset Value and make a company seem more desirable than it really is. To avoid this, I recommend subtracting both Liabilities and Intangible Assets from Total Assets to arrive at a more accurate Net Asset Value. Some financial websites will do this for you, reporting figures as Tangible Net Assets.

The final important figure from the Balance Sheet is the Net Asset Value per share (NAV/share), often referred as just NAV and implying "per share." This is the amount that a shareholder would receive for each share if the company was liquidated and the assets were evenly distributed to the shareholders. We can arrive at this figure through the following calculation:

$$\text{NAV/share} = \text{NAV} / \text{Shares Outstanding}$$

It's impossible to indicate what a "good" NAV/share looks like because financials vary from company to company, but you can figure that higher NAV/share are more desirable. A high NAV/share indicates that the company is making more money than its spending, which is vital for long-term success.

Moving on from the Balance Sheet, the Income Statement lists the Revenue and the Earnings/Income. There's a slight difference between Earnings and Income, but for our purposes we can consider them to be the same. I'll use the term Earnings over Income moving forward. Revenue corresponds to the money that a company earns through its business. Earnings are obtained by subtracting the cost of running the business from the Revenue. The income statement of a healthy company will show the revenue and earnings increasing in tandem.

The Cash Flow Statement summarizes the amount of money that a company receives from its business, investments, and every other source of income minus its Liabilities. A company's ability to generate cash is one of the most important criteria in deciding the health of the company. Cash flow should be reviewed and compared on a yearly basis because seasonal variations occur depending on the type of business.

There are many companies — namely, digital startups — that have a diminishing or nonexistent cash flow. These are commonly technology companies that spend all of their money on research and marketing. These companies often finance their business by borrowing, issuing stock, or partnering with an established financial partner. I strongly advise against investing in such companies. Overall, it's safer to buy seasoned companies with growing earnings and positive cash flow. There are, however, exceptions to this rule. Some startups with no initial cash flow become big winners — look no further than Facebook. Understand that Facebook is not the norm; there are many startup, cash-less companies that go under for every Facebook that succeeds. When the internet was first being developed for commercial use around 1994, every Tom, Dick, and Harry began an internet-based company, creating what was known as the 'dot-com bubble.' The bubble burst in 2000, and large numbers of these companies that had no source of income went out of business.

/

Congratulations — you've made it through the nitty-gritty! Out of all the tools available for evaluating and appraising stocks, I find that the most useful ones are Price/Earnings Ratio (P/E), Price/Book, Return on Equity (ROE), and Yield. We just condensed a wealth of information into a minimal amount of space, and it will certainly take you some time to internalize all of these tools for evaluating stocks. To make your life easier, here's a table that summarizes each factor that has been previously discussed.

Evaluation Tool	Definition
Large Cap / Small Cap	**Large Cap** — Companies with a market value over $1 billion. **Small Cap** — Companies with a market value under $1 billion.
Value Stock / Growth Stock	**Value Stock** — Stocks that have solid earnings, typically with P/Es around '15.' **Growth Stock** — Stocks that are thought to have the potential to outperform the market (P/Es significantly over '15').
Price Per Share	The cost of each share of stock.
52-Week High & Low	The highest and lowest Price Per Share of a given stock over the past year. Smaller differences indicate less volatility.
Beta Value	A measure of a stock's volatility in relation to the market. A value of '1' indicates a neutral rating.
Price/Book	A measure of how much Book Value is received for buying a share of stock.
Price Per Earnings Ratio (P/E)	A measure of how much money a company is making for each share of stock.
Yield	A percentage that measures how a company's dividend compares to its Price Per Share.
Return on Equity (ROE)	A percentage that measures how well a company has used the money invested by stockholders to increase its profits.
Cash Flow	The amount of money that a company receives from its business, investments, and other income, minus its Liabilities.

The Bullet Points

- Buy American stocks over foreign stocks.

- Grow your portfolio by adding in a mixture of large cap, small cap, value, and growth stocks. The risk-averse investor should buy a greater percentage of large cap and value stocks, while the more daring investor should scout for more small cap and growth stocks.

- Focus more on the Dividend Yield than the amount of the dividend. When you're buying a stock that pays a dividend, make the transaction before the ex-dividend date. When you're selling a stock that pays a dividend, make the transaction after the record date.

- The metrics discussed in this chapter can help you find good investments. For stocks in my taxable account, I find that the most useful ones are P/E and ROE. For stocks in my retirement account, I pay special attention to P/E and Yield. In Chapter 8, I'll discuss taxable and retirement accounts and explain why some investments perform better in one account over another.

4

LESSONS FROM THE PIT

Prior to the digital era in which trading is done electronically, stock trades were made by hand signals and shouting from pits, areas on the floor of the stock exchange. These pits were epicenters for investing knowledge. Stockbrokers working in the pit didn't focus on theoretical information; they saw the effects of actual transactions.

Novice investors don't have the luxury of gaining this first-hand experience, which puts us at a disadvantage. I hope to minimize that disadvantage by highlighting the best and worst investment decisions over the course of my 50+ year career. Let's first turn to the bad ones and see what we can learn from my mistakes.

/

My Mistakes

For the most part, I've run into trouble when I've tried to outsmart the market by buying and selling individual stocks. I was never a frequent trader, but I think I'd be much further ahead if I invested more money in the S&P 500 and DIA index funds, committing to never sell a share unless I needed cash. Nature being what it is, and because of my competitive spirit, I ended up buying individual companies and ETFs. I also didn't have the best framework for making these investments, as I didn't know what I was looking at when I checked under the hood. My decision to buy a stock or an ETF was often based on what I heard on TV or read in a financial publication.

This is all to say: stick to the strategy of keeping a solid index fund as the backbone of your portfolio and make sure to have valid reasons for buying a company.

Suntech Power Holdings (STP)

One of my worst mistakes was buying Suntech Power Holdings, a Chinese company that manufactured solar panels. I was motivated to buy the stock because China, which had a population of 1.3 billion at the time, had publicly announced that it wanted to convert home heating to solar. When I researched the company, I found that it had good earnings and analysts had given it a positive recommendation in spite of its high P/E, which was well above '40.'

On 12/28/07, I bought Suntech for $84.77 per share. Soon after I made the purchase, the stock price went into freefall. By the end of January 2008, the price was $53.02. I reasoned that if the stock was worth buying at $84.77, it was an even better buy at $53.02; I doubled down on Suntech and bought more shares. During 2008 and 2009 I sold calls (I'll explain selling calls in Chapter 9) and recouped a small amount of my investment. Sometime thereafter, Suntech had to restate its earnings; the earnings had not been reported correctly, and the bottom fell out of the stock. By July 2011, the stock was selling for $7.34. During the years before and after 2011, analysts' recommendations projected higher stock prices than the current price, so I continued to hold my shares. But the analysts were wrong; the stock soon became worthless, and I lost my entire investment.

Let's take a minute to consider what mistakes I made in this story.

1. I shouldn't have bought a company headquartered in a foreign country where reporting standards may not be up to the standards of the United States.
2. I should have been more wary of Suntech's high P/E. Stocks with high P/Es can tumble quickly if earnings don't keep accelerating.
3. I should have sold my shares when the stock dropped by almost 40% in less than 6 months.
4. I shouldn't have compounded my loss by buying more shares. When a stock drops precipitously, don't try to make up for the loss by buying more shares.

Instead, cut the bleeding and sell; early losses are
better than big losses later on.

5. I shouldn't have held my stock when it dropped to
single digits. At the time, my thinking was that I
didn't have much to lose, as the price was so low in
comparison to what I paid for it. But if a company is
performing that poorly, its likelihood of rebounding
is pretty low.

In golf, there's a saying that if you hit the ball in the rough,
just chip out. Don't try to be a hero and attempt a difficult
shot to make up for your mistake. Doing so will likely put
you deeper in the rough.

Transocean (RIG)

My investment in Transocean, a deep water gas and oil
drilling company, represents one of my classic mistakes. In
April 2010, an explosion occurred on one of Transocean's
drilling platforms in the Gulf of Mexico, resulting in eleven
deaths. Prior to the explosion, Transocean's stock sold as high
as $101.40. But by 2011, the stock had dropped 50%, as
responsibility for the explosion had not been determined.
There was talk that Transocean's insurance might not cover
the loss, which would decimate the company financially. I
thought that the stock would rebound, leading me to buy
more shares in September 2011 for $59.29. I could not have
been more wrong: the stock price continued to sink. By
October 2015, I gave up on Transocean and sold my shares

for $15.83, a 74% loss. Recently, the stock was selling for $4.24.

While I couldn't have foreseen the disaster that occurred on the Transocean drilling platform, my subsequent actions were riddled with mistakes.

1. I should have respected the extent to which a disastrous event can impact a company. With responsibility not determined after the explosion, there was no limit as to what Transocean might have to pay.
2. I shouldn't have bought additional shares with a sinking price.
3. Once bought, I held the stock way too long after the price continued to fall. If a stock drops more than 10% from your purchase price, it's time to reassess your reasons for holding it.
4. I shouldn't have made financial decisions based on the hope that the company's fortunes would turn around. Hope alone doesn't save a troubled company.

Boeing (BA)

An example of what happens to a company when it faces a significant misfortune is happening to Boeing, the world's leader in building commercial aircraft. I don't own Boeing, but it offers a good lesson about investing in a company that has had a fundamental problem with its business.

Boeing built a new plane, the 737MAX, which had a design fault. The new model crashed on two occasions, killing all of the passengers on board, and the plane was grounded until the fault could be determined. This mandate meant that Boeing had to cut back on selling planes, affecting Boeing's bottom line. It also subjected Boeing to possible insurance liability, just like Transocean. Boeing's stock is now down from its high of $439 to about $335, a loss of about 25%. Time will tell which way the stock price is heading. Some investors may see an opportunity in a company like Boeing, but I'd be cautious about investing in companies that are facing major problems.

Ambarella (ABA)

Ambarella makes high-definition video compressor units for body cameras. I became aware of the company on a ski trip in 2015 where I saw skiers tearing down the mountain with GoPro cameras mounted to their helmets. Checking further, I found that Ambarells's processors were used not only in sports cameras, but in police body cameras. In January 2015, the stock was selling for $50.67, and I bought shares in June 2015 for $104.62 per share. When the cameras were no longer the craze of sports fans, orders for Ambarella's processor took a nose-dive, as did Ambarella's stock price. I continued to hold the stock for two more years, during which I lessened my cost by a few dollars by selling some calls (I'll explain selling calls in a later chapter). Feeling that the company offered a good product, I hoped that the stock would rebound within these two years, but I was proven wrong. I finally sold my shares in March 2016 for $37.93, a 63% loss. Recently, Ambarella was selling for $58; it never again reached the high where I bought.

Let's round up my mistakes...

1. I had no business buying a stock that had doubled in price within six months. Earnings rarely justifies such a price increase; in other words, the value of Ambarella was inflated when I made the transaction. I can't recall the P/E when I bought Ambarella, but it must have been sky-high.
2. I should have realized that stocks that shoot up quickly can fall just as fast. Ambarella was a volatile investment, and I should have kept a closer watch on the falling price to minimize my loss. Always be wary of crazes; they can go out of style quickly.

There's a natural tendency to avoid selling a stock for a loss, largely because it forces us to admit that we've made a mistake. Forget such a tendency, and be objective. Confront your stocks as a professional gambler confronts blackjack. For the gambler, there's no money on the table; there's just chips. The professional makes decisions — when to ask for another card, hold, double down, or take insurance — based on what provides the best chance of winning. The amount of money on the table or whether the gambler is ahead or behind does not impact his decision. Above all else, a true professional knows when to cut his losses and walk away.

Fannie Mae (FNMA) and Freddie Mac (FMCC)

My failed investments in Fannie Mae (FNMA) and Freddie Mac (FMCC) offered an important lesson in risk. Even investments that are considered safe are subject to unpredictable and even catastrophic events.

FNMA and FMCC were Government Sponsored Enterprises (GSE) in the business of financing home loans. Though the government sponsored these organizations, it wasn't necessarily responsible for their potential failures. At the time, the government wanted to incentivize home ownership, so it encouraged FNMA and FMCC to make loans to people who were not prime borrowers. When the financial crisis hit in 2007 and 2008, these less-than-stellar borrowers defaulted on their mortgage payments. The lenders — that is, the banks — seized control over the defaulted homes and tried to sell them in an effort to recoup the money lent to the borrowers. But because so many borrowers defaulted all at once, the value of homes plummeted and the lenders couldn't sell for a good price. They had no choice but to eat their losses, and the lenders fell into a black hole. FNMA and FMCC went down with them.

FNMA and FMCC ended up losing so much money that they had to declare bankruptcy. Once again, the government didn't claim responsibility for these failures even though it had sponsored FNMA and FMCC. Those who invested in FNMA and FMCC — including yours truly — had no choice but to take it on the chin. I held onto my shares for several years after the bankruptcy, hoping that the government would step in and that the stock would rebound. Neither happened. Eventually, I sold my shares for 50 cents on the dollar, a 50% loss.

Now, what were my mistakes?

1. I shouldn't have assumed that government sponsored enterprises (GSEs) were risk-proof. Although I knew that FNMA and FMCC weren't formal agencies of the government, I thought that the government had a moral, if not legal responsibility to prevent them from bankruptcy. Obviously, I was wrong. If something isn't written on the dotted line, it has no meaning, even if it's from the government.

2. I shouldn't have held onto an investment that had declared bankruptcy. It would have been much better to sell my stake and use whatever money I recovered for a better investment. Unfortunately, my pride got in the way.

Bear Stearns (BCA)

For much of my investing career, I didn't keep much of an eye on the 'winners' of my portfolio. But there were a few times when some of my most consistent investments suddenly fell apart. A key example is Bear Stearns, an investment banking company that unraveled in 2008. In order to understand what happened, let me provide a quick background of investment banking.

After the stock market crashed in 1929 and the Great Depression was born, the government made a number of changes designed to renew confidence in our banking system. One of those was the Glass-Steagall Act, which prohibited banks from making risky investments with the money from savings accounts. But in 1999, this act was repealed so that banks could once again offer savings accounts while making investments. Bear Stearns was an example of these investment banks. Unfortunately, many of its investments were tied into the housing market, and the bank was decimated in the 2007-2008 housing crisis. It found itself without enough cash to pay back credits, and in March of 2008, it was taken over by J.P. Morgan, another large investment bank. The shocking part about Bear Stearns was the suddenness of its collapse. In February of 2008, Bear Stearns stock traded at $93; one month later, it was down 90%.

With Bear Stearns, I can't find anything that I did wrong. Since buying the stock in 1994, the company had demonstrated consistent gains. It was a highly-respected institution, with over 15,000 employees at its peak. Bear Stearns had all the marks of a solid, large cap investment, but it simply fell apart. The lesson to be learned is that there's no such thing as a 'safe' investment, with the exception of United States Treasuries which will be discussed in Chapter 7. That being said, I could have avoided the extent of these calamities if I had allocated more money towards index funds and ETFs rather than common stocks. I also would have slept better at night.

My Successes

Now that I've sufficiently depressed myself by focusing on my mistakes, let's shift the mood and discuss my successes. This section is much more fun to write.

But before I get into the stocks that paid off for me, I want to discuss the financial decision that has been the most fruitful for me: paying off the mortgage on my home. When I first got a loan to buy my house, my father told me that I should put all of my extra cash towards my mortgage. He believed that paying off a mortgage is a way of investing in yourself, which is the best investment that you can make. I bought my home with a 7% loan from Southern California Savings and Loan (the company has since been taken over by another entity). Every time I had some extra money, I used it to pay off my mortgage until one day, I had enough to pay off the loan entirely. I clearly remember the day that I walked into the loan company to pay off my final installment.

"Why do you want to pay off such a good loan?" the woman behind the desk asked me.

"Because I want to own my own house," I responded.

There isn't a better feeling than owning your own home without a mortgage. It means that you'll always have a roof over your head, and no one can evict you. More, real estate is a terrific investment that is likely to appreciate in value. The average homeowner's most valuable asset isn't a stock or a fund, it's the home itself. The value of my home has gone up more than almost any stock I ever owned.

City National Bank (CNB) | | Royal Bank of Canada (RY)

I bought shares of City National Bank in June of 1993 (the company later became the Royal Bank of Canada). Since my office was located around the corner, I got to know Neal Genda, who handled investments for the bank's clients and managed our office's retirement account. Neal was a straight-shooter with whom I enjoyed discussing investments. When the bank's shares dropped to $4, Neal advised that he was buying more shares. I followed suit; I kept my initial investment and bought more shares over the years to come. Today, my investment in Royal Bank of Canada is worth more than one million dollars. Thanks, Neal!

This success may be perplexing, especially considering the previous sections on my mistakes. Just a moment ago, I advised you to sell your shares when a company's stock plummets — not to buy more. The only difference is that with the Royal Bank of Canada, I had access to someone on the inside. As I mentioned, none of us are permitted into the boardrooms of the companies we're investing in. But talking to an officer in charge of the investing division is about as close as you can come.

Costco (COST)

In 2000, I bought Costco at $30.36. What was my motivation, you might ask? My wife shopped there, and she noticed that the lines at the check-out counter were always long. The volume of customers piqued my interest, but I didn't invest until I looked into Costco's business model. At the time, members paid a $50 annual fee just to shop at Costco, which created a tremendous amount of revenue on top of the company's sales. Today, Costco shares are selling at more than $290, and Costco continues to be a great company. Buying Costco followed Peter Lynch's advice to buy companies that you're familiar with.

Amgen (AMGN)

Earlier, I told you the story about how I came to buy shares of Amgen through my statistician, who decided that she had no time to help me after working at the pharmaceutical giant. But, that isn't the whole story. When I first heard about Amgen, I looked further and found that it was working on a new drug that could manage or possibly cure diseases that were all but impossible to treat. Being a physician, I knew that the drugs would have a huge market if they indeed worked. I initially bought 300 shares of Amgen in 1999 at $9.02. Through subsequent purchases, stock splits, and my refusal to ever sell a share, I now have 1,000 shares of the company. At the time of this writing, Amgen is trading at $196.

Apple (APPL)

Apple is another success story. I started buying Apple in 2007 when shares sold for $24.79. Every time that I walked through the mall, the Apple store had a line out the door. I also really liked Apple products. It wasn't long before I replaced my Microsoft computer with an Apple and purchased an iPhone and an iPad. Apple is now selling for about $230 per share, and it's bound to go up given its popularity.

I don't want to gloat any further — let's take a look at the bullet points.

/

The Bullet Points

- Buy companies headquartered in the United States.

- Be wary of buying companies with a P/E greater than 25.

- Sell your shares if a stock drops precipitously, a calamity hits the company, or a stock has an ongoing loss greater than the market.

- Absorbing a loss early is better than suffering a greater loss later.

- Your first mistake is the cheapest one; subsequent mistakes are more expensive.

- Make decisions based on analysis, not on how much money you're ahead or behind.

- The best investment you can make is owning your own home without a mortgage.

- When making a decision to buy or sell a stock, rely on your own judgment. It's OK to solicit the opinions of others who might have knowledge about a company, but don't waste time listening to people who spout off as if they're experts on every company in the market.

- Don't flagellate yourself over every loss. Not every investment that loses money is the result of your mistake. Bad things can happen to good companies, and these events can be unpredictable. When this happens, keep your chin up and move on.

- If the company is developing a new product like a drug, try to determine if that product will have wide-spread appeal and use. You may need to consult others that have more knowledge about the company and its products.

- Unless you need money, never sell a share as long as the business is going in the right direction.

GENERAL UPKEEP: BUILDING A BOAT TO LAST

If you keep a top-of-the line Mercedes in your driveway without protecting it from the elements, it won't be long until the paint begins to dull, the tires deflate, and the car's value decreases. Your investment portfolio is exactly the same. Without care and upkeep, it will fall apart. Luckily for you, the strategy suggested in this book is committed to long-term investing. That corresponds to a minimal amount of work on your end, as we won't be making frequent trades at key moments. But that doesn't mean that you can kick up your feet and forget about your investments after you make the transaction. Complacency is the biggest mistake that a novice investor can make after entering the market.

Keep an Eye on your Companies

In Chapter 4, we talked about the tools that you can use to find companies that are ripe for your investment dollars. But just because a company seems like a good investment in one moment doesn't mean that it will remain that way. Your reason for holding a stock can become obsolete because of evolving industries and technologies, or because management fails to recognize changes in the business environment.

Blockbuster, a video rental company, is a classic example of how a company failed to change with the times. Before the prevalence of video streaming, Blockbuster was the single titan in the video rental business. It was almost impossible to drive through any town in America without seeing a Blockbuster video rental store. The company rented out DVDs of movies and television series, which people could watch in the comfort of their own homes. No one could compete with them because their inventory was so impressive.

It goes without saying that Blockbuster was a smart investment during the 1990s and the early 2000s. At its peak, the company had over 9,000 stores worldwide, more than 85,000 employees, and a valuation of over $5 billion. Then, everything changed.

One day, a Silicon Valley investor named Reed Hastings decided to rent the movie *Apollo 13* from his local Blockbuster. Who knows if he ever got around to watching the film, but he forgot to return it on time and ended up racking up $40 in late fees. Late fees were a major part of Blockbuster's revenue stream; in 2000, they collected nearly $800 million in late fees. The penalty, as well as a number of changing factors in the marketplace, motivated Mr. Hastings to start a company called Netflix.

The early Netflix is pretty much unrecognizable from the company we all know today. There was no app, no original content, and no streaming service. The company started out with a commitment to DVDs. Rather than making the customer drive to their nearest Blockbuster, Netflix mailed the customer a DVD of the movie that they wanted to watch. Once the customer finished watching, he or she would pop it back in the mail and Netflix would mail the next movie in the customer's docket. Netflix didn't have any fancy technology; it was simply a rental company designed to eliminate late fees.

In 2000, Reed Hastings walked into Blockbuster's corporate offices with the intent of selling his young company for $50 million. The executives of Blockbuster practically laughed him out of the room. Fast forward thirteen years, Blockbuster couldn't compete with Netflix. Its business fell off a cliff, and by 2010, Blockbuster stock was trading at 17 cents a share. This meant that the company was valued at $37 million, quite a come-down from its former valuation of $5 billion. Soon thereafter, Blockbuster declared bankruptcy and closed down its stores. Netflix went in the other direction, ascending to the pinnacle of the entertainment business and revolutionizing the way that we consume content.

When you peel back the layers of the story, it becomes clear that Blockbuster and Netflix were trying to do the exact same thing: maximize profits by renting movies and television shows. But their philosophies on achieving success were polar opposites. While Blockbuster believed in a traditional model and the value of brick and mortar stores, Netflix saw that consumers wanted a more convenient option that eliminated late fees. That insight led to a model that disrupted the industry and doomed Blockbuster to bankruptcy.

This story has a lot to teach the amateur investor. Looking into the past, it seems obvious that Netflix had a much keener sense of the market than Blockbuster. But as investors, we don't have the benefit of hindsight. Rather, our success hinges on our ability to predict the future. There was a time in the late 1990s when I probably would have recommended buying Blockbuster stock. But at some point, as video streaming technology and competitors like Netflix emerged, the rationale for investing in Blockbuster became moot. When you can justify your decision with sound reasoning, it's time to sell.

This probably sounds much easier said than done. How are we supposed to stay on top of our portfolios and evaluate the health of the companies we've invested in? I recommend taking the following steps:

Read the news.

It's important to know what's going on with the companies that you've invested in. Otherwise, you're like a pilot who knew where he was when he took off but is now flying blind.

If you only have a few stocks, the easiest way to stay updated on their performance is to use Google. Type in the name of the company followed by "recent news," and the search engine will give you the latest stories affecting the company. Most of the time, the news about a company will be routine happenings and nothing of great import. But sometimes, you'll find something significant. It's impossible to look for one single thing as the nature of business varies so much from company to company, but the headlines will give you a general insight into what the company has been doing as of late. Developments such as product releases, lawsuits or scandals, and leadership changes are particularly important. Look out for sudden changes in the stock price, especially in relation to the general trend of the SPY and DIA funds.

As your portfolio becomes more diverse, I recommend using a financial app to track the performances of your stocks. There are countless programs that allow you to enter the name of the stock, the date you bought the stock, and the amount you paid. Once you've inputted the information, the app will track real-time data. These evolving reports can allow you to keep an eye on your investments with minimal effort.

Now that I've told you how to stay abreast of your stocks, I want to encourage you to do so on a routine basis. When you first buy a stock, you'll probably check the price pretty frequently. However, once the newness wears off, there is a tendency to "put it in the closet" so to speak and not look at the stock for prolonged stretches of time. That's a mistake:

good and bad things can happen when you're not watching. Here's what I want you to do: pick a time every week to check your stocks, read about the companies (you're a partial owner, after all), and keep a record of the date and value of your portfolio. I promise you that your time will be well-spent.

Review financial reports.

To reiterate from Chapter 3, financial reports are long, arduous, and boring. But they include kernels that can be tremendously valuable to the investor. You should pay attention to the following components of the report in particular:

- **Report to Shareholders** — written by the CEO and often outlines the company's plan for the future.
- **Balance Sheet** — indicates a company's Assets versus its Liabilities. Be wary of any dramatic spikes in Liabilities.
- **Income Statement** — indicates how much a company is earning. You want earnings to be increasing year after year. If earnings go down, you should look further. Is this a temporary dip because the company puts more money into research and development, or is it a red flag indicating a structural change affecting the company's business?
- **Cash Flow** — indicates how much money the company has to operate its business. Cash flow is the mother's milk of a company's business.

Scout for competitors and threats.

A company only remains valuable if it continues to offer a better service or better products than its competitors. Rest assured that there will always be new ventures committed to disrupting existing businesses. For every Uber, there's a Lyft; for every Microsoft, there's an Apple; and for every General Motors, there's a Tesla. As Warren Buffet said, buy companies that have an economic moat that protects them from competitors.

If you find a competitor that poses a significant threat to your company, educate yourself on the differences between your investment and the competitor. Are the companies targeting the same audience? How do their marketing initiatives compare? How is each company adapting to the modern shifts and trends? If you feel like your company is losing ground to one of these competitors, you may want to consider selling your stock.

Competing companies aren't the only threat to look out for. Emerging technologies, new laws, and social movements can drastically impact the value of a company. Take a look at corporations like ExxonMobil, a leading power in the oil and fossil fuel industry. ExxonMobil has been a titan for decades, but current events may pose a significant threat to its business. Global warming and other environmental factors are growing all the more prevalent with each passing day, posing a significant concern for ExonnMobil's core business. Investors interested in the fuel industry may opt to invest in other companies focused on producing clean energy. Exxon-Mobil's stock price doesn't suffer from an oil shortage, but from an oil glut that depresses the price of oil. It's also affected by a transformation of drivers from gas-powered to electric cars.

While monitoring your companies may seem like a hassle at first, I can promise that it will become second-nature over time. It doesn't require that much time or energy; it just requires discipline. I can't stress the importance of taking a broad overview of your investments a few times a year. It could be the difference between draining your money in a company like Blockbuster and making a killing through the success of Netflix.

Contribute to your Portfolio on a Scheduled Basis

Hopefully, I've made a compelling case that investing leads to long-term wealth. The more money that you invest, the more valuable your portfolio will become. That means that you should be contributing to your portfolio as much as you can, without cutting into the 'nest egg' that you should set aside for unexpected emergencies.

I've found two particularly effective strategies that make it easy to continue growing investment portfolios.

Dividend Reinvestment Programs

As you may recall from Chapter 3, dividends are payments that a company distributes to its shareholders. Rather than pocketing that money, you can pump it back into your investment portfolio through a Dividend Reinvestment Program (DRP). A Dividend Reinvestment Program allows you to compound the value of your dividends by reinvesting all dividends to buy additional shares of the issuing company. Compounding, in financial terms, means reinvesting the money from an investment to earn more money.

Once your dividends are reinvested to buy additional shares of a company, future dividend payments become based on the now increased number of shares. More often than not, the dividend will only buy a fraction of a share. That's okay; fractional shares will add up to whole shares over time. An additional advantage of a Dividend Reinvestment Program is that it allows you to increase your number of shares in most companies without paying a fee to your brokerage. Because the dividend is added directly by the company without a brokerage, you aren't subject to typical charges.

If a company offers a Dividend Reinvestment Program, I recommend enrolling in it when you buy your shares. Unfortunately many companies don't have Dividend Reinvestment Programs. You'll scarcely find DRPs for exchange traded funds or index funds because they include many companies. That being said, many brokerages will reinvest your dividends even if the company itself doesn't have a DRP. When you buy a stock, tell your broker that you want all dividends reinvested and check to see if they charge a commission for doing so. The full-service brokerage that I use, Wells Fargo Advisors, reinvests all of my dividends without any charge.

One final point before I go into examples of how dividend reinvestment works: although you don't receive the dividend as cash, the dividend is still considered income that must be reported to the IRS at tax time. At the end of the year, the company issuing the dividend will send you a statement called a 1099, showing the amount of the dividend that must be reported to the IRS when filing your tax returns.

Let's look at some examples that show the benefit of reinvesting dividends and the power of compounding. Suppose you make the following investment in a company called XYZ:

- 100 shares
- $1 per share
- 4% annual dividend

Assuming that the stock price remains the same, the dividend will be $4.00 per year. Let's further assume that you're twenty-five years old and that you're like Rip Van Winkle...except instead of falling asleep for twenty years, you forget about the investment for forty years until you're sixty-five and ready for retirement. How much do you think your investment would be worth if you just kept your 100 shares without buying any additional ones?

If you took the $4.00 dividend each year and spent it, you'd have $100 at age sixty-five (that's the principal value of your investment: 100 shares x $1). If you took the $4.00 dividend and put it in a piggy bank, you'd have $100 + $160 (40 x $4.00), or a total of $260. Now, if you had the money in a Dividend Reinvestment Program (DRP) and the money compound each year until you were sixty-five at the 4% annual rate, you'd end up with $480 (excluding cents).

Spend the Dividend: $100
Save Dividend in Piggy Bank: $260
With DRP, Compounding Annual Interest: $480

Now, let's add another ingredient: each year, you buy an additional $100 of the stock (we're holding the stock price steady), and the stock continues to pay a 4% dividend. If you spent the dividend, you'd have $4,000 (40 x $100); if you put the dividend in your piggy bank, you'd have $4,160 ($4,000 + $160). Now comes the big one. If you had the stock in a dividend reinvestment program, your investment would be worth $10,362.

Spend the Dividend: $4,000
Save Dividend in Piggy Bank: $4,160
With DRP, Compounding Annual Interest: $10,362

The numbers speak for themselves. And remember, I held the stock price steady in these examples. In real life, the stock price would most likely be going up, meaning that the 4% dividend would generate even more income for you. If you're interested in calculating returns for compounding interest, you can find online calculators through a quick Google search.

Now, let's take a close look at two real-life investments that utilized dividend reinvestment programs. In October of 1967, I was gifted twenty-five shares of Combined Insurance, which later changed its name to AON. At the time that I acquired the stock, it was selling for $64.37, equating to a total value of $1,609.37. The stock was put into a dividend reinvestment program. Fifty-one years later, my initial investment had grown to 813.80 shares with a market value of $132,698. I had similar success with my investment in Occidental Petroleum (OXY). In March of 1966, I bought twenty-eight shares for $1,347.50, and the stock was similarly placed in a DRP. Fifty-two years later, I found myself with 1,446.7 shares worth $93,702. These investments increased in value because of stock splits, stock price increases, dividend reinvestment programs, and compounding interest.

The results are glaring: enroll in dividend reinvestment programs where compounding can do its magic.

Dollar Cost Averaging

Dollar cost averaging, often referred to as dollar averaging, is an investment strategy that centers around budgeting. The investor commits to two things: a sum to invest, and a set interval at which that investment will occur. With dollar averaging, you buy a stock on a designated date regardless of the stock price. The dollars that you commit will buy more shares when the price is down and fewer shares when the price is higher. This strategy takes market watching and market volatility out of the picture. Dollar averaging is an excellent way to invest and accumulate shares in a company or fund. I find that dollar averaging works best for index funds, including the S&P 500 and the DIA fund. By dollar averaging the S&P 500 or the DJIA fund, you don't need to follow the price of the stock or worry about reading up on a company. Instead, you can continually increase your investment by betting on the United States economy, which is the best bet that you can make.

The amount and the interval of your dollar averaging investments depend on your income and your expenses. That being said, you should plan on investing the same amount of money at your pre-set intervals. If unexpected costs prevent you from contributing your planned amount, buy shares with whatever money you can afford. The important point is to keep accumulating shares over time. When you're young and your funds are limited, I suggest an investing interval of every three months, say on the first business day of each quarter. It isn't a bad idea to place your money earmarked for investment in a brokerage savings account. Then, instruct your broker to buy the shares with the dollar amount you select on the day you designate. The brokerage will make the purchase automatically, eliminating any decision-making on your part. If necessary, you can always instruct your broker to modify the amount.

Evaluate your Advisers

As your portfolio grows and you become a more established investor, you'll want to take a close look at the fees that you're paying your financial advisers. Because fees are automatically deducted either as a percent of the value of your portfolio or as a cost for every transaction, it's easy to not notice how much you're forking over to the specialists working on your account. Even though your investment fees aren't deducted from your savings account and don't show up on your credit card statement, it's still money that you're spending. With that in mind, we should all take extra efforts to ensure we're paying a fair amount.

If you recall from Chapter 1, the brokerage type of your choice will determine how much you pay. Full-service brokerages allow you to gain the advice of a professional, while discount brokerages empower you to make your own trades. You can also enroll in guided investing programs, where your portfolio is handled by a team of professionals who buy a mixture of stocks, bonds, and funds. This option is easily the most expensive, as it requires the care and attention of experienced analysts.

If you're using a discount brokerage, you can rest assured that you aren't paying exorbitant fees (just make sure that the brokerage is charging you the appropriate rate of $5 to $10 per transaction). However, if you have a full-service brokerage or a guided investment account, I suggest comparing the growth of your investment to "the market" — that is, the SPY and DIA funds. Ask yourself: is my account doing better or worse than the stock market as a whole? If the answer is considerably worse, it may be time to put your money somewhere else. After all, if you're paying for a qualified professional, he or she should be able to beat the market. Using the SPY and DIA funds as the benchmark for the value of your investment is very simple. Just select a certain time period — I suggest evaluating in 1-year and 5-year terms — and compare the percent change of your portfolio to that of the SPY and DIA funds.

Finally, don't overlook the value of having a trusted adviser who gives you the time of day. Even if you're a small potato investor, you deserve the full attention of a qualified professional. If your adviser is difficult to reach or connect with, you should find someone else. After all, this is your hard-earned money on the line; you should feel confident in the person or people managing it.

Start an Investment Club

When I recommend starting an investment club, I'm not talking about the type of club where people sit in a circle and talk about dry topics over a platter of stale crackers. A good investment club will produce results that benefit all of the members' financial health. If the adage, "Two heads are better than one" is true, imagine what a club of several driven people with a common incentive can accomplish.

I've been a member of the same investment club for over

twenty-five years. I've learned far more from my investment club than I ever would have learned as an individual investor, largely because the club has pooled the knowledge and efforts of people with diverse ideas. Being a part of the club has also been a financially successful experience.

There's some flexibility in how your investment club can operate, but I recommend the following stipulations. The club should have four to eight members. With fewer than four, the club becomes a chat session, and with more than eight, you lose individual participation. Each member should contribute a set amount — say $500 — to start the club. An additional amount — something in the ballpark of $100 — should be contributed every three months. Of course the amounts can vary depending on the earnings of the members. The club should meet at a set date and time, ideally on a monthly basis.

Ideally, the club should have at least the number of stocks as there are members so that each member can be responsible for following a company. At meetings, each member should report on news of their assigned company, followed by a recommendation of whether the company should be held or sold. Other club members should be able to challenge this recommendation; after a healthy debate, the members vote on whether the club should hold, sell, or buy more shares of the company in question. After everyone has reviewed their assigned holdings, members should pitch new investments for the club to consider.

Here's a list of guidelines to keep in mind for investment clubs:

- Keep your membership around the size of a basketball team: four to eight people is ideal. Having too many people will limit each member's participation.
- Encourage every club member to have equal participation.
- Forge a commitment to consistent meeting dates.
- Use a spreadsheet to keep track of the club's holdings. Your tracking system should include each stock held by the club, the price per share, the present value, and the change from the prior month.
- If a member wants to leave the club, he or she should be entitled to an equal share of the club's value. The club may need to sell some stocks to pay the departing member his or her share.
- Keep minutes and notes of the club.
- The decision to buy or sell shares of stocks or funds should be determined by majority vote.

Once you've established your club's rules and members, you can formalize your investment club as a business entity. This entails creating bylaws and a name registered with the state to open a brokerage account and submit taxes. You'll also need to hire an accountant to file tax returns and advise on the setup of the club. Most likely, you'll form a subchapter S-corporation so that each member receives individual tax returns and the club itself is not taxed. Setting up your club may sound like a pain, but the benefits are very much worth the paperwork.

Develop a Top-Notch Record-Keeping Strategy

While your brokerage house keeps records, you should always be aware of your investments. I recommend enrolling in an online program that keeps track of your holdings. I personally use Yahoo Finance, which automatically tracks the performance of my portfolio. It's easy to create an account with this program, and it's an invaluable tool. Each time that you make a transaction in the stock market, indicate the company, the price per share, and the number of shares purchased or sold. The program will do everything else for you.

Remember that good investing isn't marked by genius or talent; it's marked by discipline, organization, research, and sound record-keeping. If you keep track of your portfolio in this way, you'll be able to make informed decisions throughout your investing career.

Cashing Out: Flag-Stop Indications for When to Sell

In Alaska, there's a flag-stop train that travels through the back-country. The train exists so that people living in the wilderness can get to and from civilization to buy supplies, see a doctor, or take care of other necessities. While en-route, the train has no scheduled stops, so passengers must raise a flag to notify the engineer to stop at the right destination. Your investment portfolio can be likened to that train. While you're moving along, a flag will appear every so often that tells you, the engineer, to stop. As is evident from my mistakes in Chapter 4, it's key to sell a stock when you discover an intrinsic problem with the company. After all, a profit isn't a profit until there's money in the bank.

Here are some of the red flags indicating that it might be time to sell a stock in your portfolio:

The fundamentals of the company have changed.

Businesses are constantly evolving based on technology, consumer trends, and the market. Just because a company starts a certain way doesn't mean it won't change. If your company has undergone a fundamental shift that impacts performance, you may want to consider selling.

New technology makes the company's product obsolete.

Look no further than Blockbuster to see the importance of technology on the stock market. We're in the midst of a technological explosion, and many companies are bound to bite the dust. Would it be smart to keep an investment in a manufacturer of home telephones? Probably not, considering that the majority of the population is substituting cell phones for landlines.

Your reasons for buying the company are no longer valid.

Whenever you buy a stock, you should have ambitious, albeit reasonable goals for that investment. As you've learned by now, there aren't two stocks made alike; each one offers distinct value to your investment. If your reason for owning a stock is no longer valid, you should consider selling.

For example, let's say that you buy a high-yield stock in order to collect dividends. If management decides to reduce or even stop the dividend altogether, you have no business owning that stock. In this scenario, management would probably use a lot of fluff to explain the loss of the dividend, but don't be influenced by such rhetoric. Any time that a company reduces or eliminates a dividend, it means the company anticipates less profit, and it's a red flag.

The Price Per Share spikes and you're anticipating a steep drop.

Now, if you're lucky enough to own a stock that has gone up like a rocket, sell half. Stocks that shoot up usually do so because of a new "hot product." When the newness wears off, they tend to fall just as fast. By selling half, you ensure that you'll capitalize on some of the profit if the stock drops. If the stock continues to rise, you'll still own shares, allowing you to benefit from the upside. I call this strategy halving the double.

Your stock has lost 10% of its value in a steady market.

If your stock has experienced a swift and sudden drop, you should critically evaluate what's happening with the company. As we've discussed, every company is destined to go through periods of decline. The key is to ensure that your company isn't an outlier.

For instance, let's say that you notice your stock in a food distribution company has taken a turn for the worse. I would recommend taking a look at the recent trends of comparable food distribution companies. If they're all on a downward trend, there's a good chance that the food distribution sector is going through a slump. In that case, you may want to hold onto the stock, keeping a close eye on the company's performance over the coming months. But if the food distribution sector is surging and your stock is falling, then something is wrong with your individual holding. It may be worthwhile to sell.

Selling a stock to cut your losses is never fun because it means accepting loss. However, this is a vital part of investing. Don't let stubbornness compound your losses! To protect yourself from significant dips in a stock's price, you can always put a 'stop order' (aka 'limit order') on a stock. We touched on these in Chapter 1, but to refresh your memory, limit orders limit your maximum loss by automatically selling your stock once it reaches a certain price.

You need cash (for something worthwhile!)

What good is money if it isn't spent? I would never encourage you to sell a stock to pay for a vacation, but there will be times in your life when you need to make significant purchases. The big kicker is acquiring the money for a down payment on a home. Especially in today's market, it's getting harder and harder for first-time homeowners to buy property. If your portfolio is valuable enough to get you into a home of your own, then I recommend jumping at the opportunity. Like I've mentioned, owning a home is a better investment than any stock in the market.

Sometimes, it can be tempting to liquidate an investment by selling a stock. Perhaps a spike in the market has you thinking about how nice it would be to collect your earnings, or a tough week in the market has dealt a blow to the value of your stock. More often than not, my advice is to refrain from selling; after all, that's the key to long-term investing. I want to note two particularly common scenarios in which you should hold your stock:

- You're tired of looking at the stock
- You feel you can make more money with another stock

Whenever these reasons pop up in my investment club, other members are quick to strike them down. Why are these bad motivators for selling? Well, they tend to be based on emotion, not logic. Before you sell, you must have a clear reason rooted in the company's fundamentals. A good discipline is to write down your reasoning for selling on a piece of paper, tuck that note into a drawer, and revisit it in a day or so. The stock price won't change that much, and waiting a few days will give you time to rethink or confirm your decision.

It's perfectly natural to want to veer away from 'boring' stocks that aren't discussed in the media and don't have any dramatic increases. But the stocks that steadily outperform the market year after year tend to be the best investments. Remember: your goal isn't to get rich quick; it's to end up with a comfortable retirement fund over the course of several decades. Don't be blinded by what constitutes real value in the stock market; the tortoise always beats the hare.

You probably don't remember the musical *Show Boat*. In that show, there is a famous song that has long been considered one of the greatest songs ever written: "Ol' Man River." One of the lines in the song is, "But ol' man river he keeps rolling along." Follow these investment strategies, and your portfolio will be just like Ol' Man River; it will keep rolling along, and one day you'll wake up and find yourself with a handsome nest egg.

The Bullet Points

- Monitor the companies that you've invested in by reading the news, reviewing financial reports, and scouting for new threats in the marketplace.

- Contribute to your portfolio by enrolling in dividend reinvestment portfolios and setting up a dollar averaging strategy that works for you.

- Evaluate your advisers by comparing the performance of your portfolio to the S&P 500 (SPY) and the Dow Jones Industrial Average Fund (DIA). If your adviser isn't beating the market, look for someone else.

- Start an investment club that encourages you to enhance your portfolio with a group of people you can trust.

- Develop a sound record-keeping routine that allows you to keep track of your investments. I recommend keeping key measurables in a spreadsheet, adding information on a semi-annual basis.

- Consider selling your stock if the fundamentals of the company have changed, new technology makes the company's product obsolete, your reasons for buying the company are no longer valid, the price per share experiences an irrational spike, your stock has lost 10% of its value in a steady market, or you need cash for a necessary expense.

6

STOCKS OF A DIFFERENT BREED

By now, you have all the knowledge that you need to tear up the world of common stocks. Worry not — there's still more to learn. As discussed early on, common stocks are ideal for the young, amateur investor with the time and luxury to invest over the long-term. However, as you become older and more experienced, you'll want to diversify your portfolio with investments other than common stocks. In this chapter, I'm going to break down three types of investments that are worth discussing:

- Mutual Funds
- Preferred Stocks
- Master Limited Partnerships (MLPs)

Mutual Funds: Here Comes the Stagecoach

In the old West, before there were trains and paved roads, it was up to the Pony Express to transport mail and packages. The cowboys of the Pony Express would gallop from station to station until their horse was worn out. Then, they'd hop on a fresh mount and repeat the cycle until they reached their destination. There was only one problem with this model: a single horse could only carry so much weight. The system didn't work for transporting heavy loads like boxes of goods. Enter stagecoaches, which were pulled by a team of horses. While these may have been slower, they made it possible to move all sorts of goods across the West. Why am I mentioning all of this? If common stocks are a series of individual horses zipping across the West, mutual funds are the stagecoaches.

Metaphors aside, a mutual fund is a type of investment that pools your dollars into a diverse array of assets. Mutual funds invest in all kinds of things including common stocks, bonds, treasuries, CDs, commodities, real estate — literally anything that can be bought or sold in a market. Some mutual funds limit their investments to one kind of asset, while others combine different types of assets. Mutual funds can take many forms, but they're distinguished by the fact that all investment decisions are made by mutual fund managers. In this regard, you can think of mutual funds as more intense versions of a full-service brokerage that you rely on for investment advice. You, the investor, have no input into how the fund is being managed. You won't confer with your mutual fund manager, and you won't be consulted before trades are made on behalf of the fund. You're simply along for the ride.

For some, this passive role is a plus. It means you don't need to make investing decisions, and you don't need to keep track of a bunch of stocks. There's also less paperwork come tax-time. Mutual fund paperwork is handled on your behalf, so you don't have to concern yourself with K1s or 1099s for each stock that you own. The only paperwork that deserves your attention are monthly and annual statements that reflect the results of the fund and the value of your investment (make sure to keep these reports for your tax preparer). Investing in mutual funds means that you get to spend your morning coffee reading the Sports section of the newspaper instead of the Business section. That being said, it's always smart to compare the results of your mutual fund to the market — that is, the SPY and DIA funds. Considering that mutual fund managers take a percentage as compensation, your mutual fund should be beating the market.

There are two fees associated with mutual funds: 1) the Ongoing Expense Ratio, which is the total fund costs divided by the total fund assets; and 2) the Load, which is a percentage of your initial investment. Expense ratios apply to every mutual fund. While rates vary, they typically range from 0.6% to 1.0%. For comparison, the expense ratio of the S&P 500 index fund is 0.19%, which is part of why I say it should be the foundation of your portfolio. A mutual fund's expense ratio covers rent, insurance, legal fees, and all the other business costs associated with running the fund. It's worth noting that the expense ratio is taken regardless of the fund's performance. In other words, you'll still be charged the expense ratio if your mutual fund loses money. You can find a mutual fund's expense ratio and investment results on the fund's prospectus.

The second type of fee, a load, is an amount that some funds charge to become a member. The load is a percentage of your initial investment, typically ranging from 2% to 5%. There are two types of loads: front-end loads, which you pay at the time you invest in the mutual fund; and back-end loads, which you pay when you sell. However, there are many 'no-load' mutual funds that don't charge a load at all. For this reason, I don't see any reason to buy a mutual fund with a load.

Mutual funds are broadly classified as being 'Open' or 'Closed.' Let's take a closer look at each:

Open Mutual Funds

In an open mutual fund, there is not a finite number of shares. That means that the total number of shares increases as people invest in the fund, and the total number of shares decreases when people leave the fund. When you join an open mutual fund, you're actually buying a percent of the fund's assets — not an actual number of shares. However, the fund then converts that percent into a number of shares, each one being worth the NAV/share. Remember — the

NAV/share is a measurement that indicates the value of a mutual fund.

You can buy an open mutual fund through your brokerage or directly from the fund itself. Buying through your brokerage, however, has limitations. Brokerages usually sell the open mutual funds that they're familiar with, so you can't be certain that your brokerage is showing you every open mutual fund that's available. Regardless of where you buy, note that most open mutual funds have a minimum investment ranging anywhere from $25 to $1,000.

Above, we discussed the costs of mutual funds — expense ratios and loads — but open mutual funds impose an extra commission to purchase the fund. Much of the time, this is a significant number, ranging from 2% to 5% of your investment. However, if you buy from the fund directly (you can purchase through the fund's website) you may be able to avoid this fee. Many mutual funds advertise that there isn't any charge to join, but definitely check the fine print — I don't believe in free lunches.

The nice thing about open mutual funds is that you don't have to buy a whole number of shares. Because these funds don't have a finite number of shares, you can contribute a flat dollar amount — $250, $1,000, $10,000 — whatever amount you like. This can be a benefit to the investor with limited funds; he or she can regularly invest small amounts on a regular schedule.

Closed Mutual Funds

Unlike open mutual funds, closed mutual funds have a finite number of shares and trade like stocks on an exchange. In other words, you can't invest a dollar amount in a closed mutual fund as you can for an open fund; you must purchase a whole number of shares.

You can use the NAV/share to determine the quality of a closed mutual fund. You can find the NAV/share of a mutual fund through any financial website, but here's the formula for the math gurus:

$$NAV/share = The\ value\ of\ the\ fund's\ holdings\ /\ Number\ of\ shares\ outstanding$$

Reading the NAV per share on its own won't tell you much; you have to compare it to the price at which the fund is trading. Here's what you need to know:

- If the price per share is greater than the NAV, the shares are trading at a premium and you should look for a different mutual fund.
- If the NAV per share is less than the price of the fund, the shares are trading at a discount; you may be getting a bargain.

As an example, take a look at the following data on Tri-Continental (TY), a closed mutual fund that has been around for 90 years and is listed on the New York Stock Exchange. On a trading day during the writing of this manuscript, TY had a NAV per share of $29.58 and traded at $26.48:

Tri-Continental (TY)
NAV/share: $29.58
Price per share: $26.48
→ For a 10.8% discount

Because the NAV per share is higher than the price per share, we can determine that TY is selling at a 10.8% discount. This discount is a benefit that doesn't apply to open mutual funds, which are always priced at the NAV/share. While buying at a discount sounds like a good thing, remember that when you sell it, the same discount may apply.

You may ask why a closed mutual fund trades above or below its NAV. There's no clear-cut answer. Like other stocks that trade with a higher or lower PE ratio, the answer relates to supply and demand, quality of management, and expectation for the future. Certain funds, such as Tri-Continental (TY), are interesting because they consistently trade at a discount.

Open or Closed — which one's for me?

My preference is that closed mutual funds are more favorable than open ones. First of all, you have the liberty to buy and sell closed funds at any moment because they're sold on the stock exchange. Open funds, on the other hand, are not traded on the exchange and are therefore more constricting. Secondly, the expense ratio of closed funds tends to be considerably less than that of open funds. Both open and closed funds are subject to management fees, but when you buy a closed fund, you're simply buying the cost of a share.

As I noted earlier, the one advantage of buying an open fund is that the beginning investor can invest small amounts of money on a regular basis, as the investor is not required to buy full shares. This is very handy when buying expensive stocks like Apple, Disney, and Google. However, I don't think that this advantage compensates for high fees and the fact that many open funds don't do as well as the market as a whole. If you're going to buy a mutual fund, I would stick to closed funds that trade at a discount.

Even though I favor closed funds over open ones, I'm not the biggest fan of mutual funds in general. I've already pointed out that the expense ratios of mutual funds are significantly higher than those of index funds. You can do just as well — probably better — investing in a stable index fund. That being said, some people are willing to pay higher fees knowing that a financial expert is handling their investments.

The Bullet Points of Mutual Funds

- Mutual funds offer a hands-off approach to investing, as your investment is managed by professionals.

- Open mutual funds allow you to invest a sum of money

rather than buying a number of shares. Closed mutual funds don't offer this privilege.

- Closed mutual funds are generally more appealing than open mutual funds because they have lower fees and can be bought and sold on the stock exchange.

- You can appraise the value of a closed mutual fund by comparing the price per share to the NAV. You want the price to be lower than the NAV!

- Avoid buying any mutual fund that charges a load! If you want to give your money away, give it to charity; you'll get more satisfaction.

/

Preferred Stocks: Stocks with a Security Blanket

If I've done my job well, you've internalized that the price of common stocks and the dividend (if any) vary based on a company's success. However, some companies — especially in the utilities and financial sectors — offer a different, more stable class of stock in addition to the common stocks that we've discussed. Such stocks are called preferred stocks. The biggest difference between common stocks and preferred stocks is that the latter have fixed dividends and fixed dates when said dividends will be paid. Because these dividends are set in stone, the price of preferred stocks are determined more by interest rates and less by the economy. Overall, preferred stocks tend to be less volatile than common stocks, and they can offset risk when implemented into your portfolio. When you buy a preferred stock, you do not become an owner of the company, and you have no voice in the running of the company. Management will not solicit your opinion, you will not be invited to the annual meeting, and you will not be asked to vote on proposals.

Coupon Rates

In order to compare preferred stocks, you need to understand coupon rates. The coupon rate is a percentage that determines a preferred stock's dividend. Higher coupon rates signify higher dividends, while lower coupon rates signify lower dividends. Keep in mind that a good coupon rate will hover around 5%. However, the important point isn't the amount of the dividend; it's the yield, which is the relationship between the amount of the dividend and how much you pay for the stock.

To determine yield, we need to account for how much the investor pays for a preferred stock. Most preferred stocks that you will encounter are priced at a par value of $25. That means that we need to compare the price of a preferred stock to $25. If the price is above $25, it will decrease your yield. On the contrary, if the price is below $25, it will drive your yield up.

This is all to say that when you're searching for preferred stocks, scout for companies with high coupon rates that are trading for less than $25 per share. Before buying shares of preferred stocks, I suggest discussing with your broker to ensure that the stock is reliable. There are several preferred stocks that have appealing coupon rates to make up for low credit ratings, and these are to be avoided.

Cumulative & Non-Cumulative Preferred Stocks

The great thing about owning preferred stocks is that the company must pay you dividends if the shareholders of common stock receive any dividend whatsoever. The dividend for preferred shares can only be stopped if the dividend for common shares is eliminated. In other words, preferred stocks have a level of protection for payment of the dividend that is not shared by common stocks. As a sweetener, some companies offer preferred shares that are cumulative. Cumulative means that if the dividend of a preferred stock is eliminated but later restored, the company must reimburse you for all dividends that have been held back. When preferred stocks are non-cumulative, the company is not on the hook to pay back dividends that have been eliminated. It goes without saying that cumulative preferred stocks are more attractive than non-cumulative ones.

Convertible Preferred Stocks

All companies that offer preferred stocks also offer common stocks. Therefore, shareholders should be able to exchange their shares of preferred stocks for common stocks, right? Well, not necessarily. Only a specific type of preferred stocks

— convertible preferred stocks — offer the ability to convert preferred shares into common shares. The vast majority of preferred stocks are not convertible.

When you're looking at a convertible preferred stock, you should examine the following factors:

- What the common shares are selling for at the time
- The exchange rate for how many common shares you would receive for every preferred share
- How much the common shares would need to sell for at the time of conversion to make the exchange worthwhile
- The date before which the conversion must occur

Convertible preferred stocks usually pay a lower dividend than a regular preferred stock because of the conversion privilege. In general, I recommend buying preferred shares for their dividend — not for a conversion privilege.

Preferred Stock Strategy

If preferred stocks are that much more stable than common stocks, why have I waited this long to discuss them? Well, remember the risk mantra: with less risk, there's less reward. It's far more difficult to build significant wealth through preferred stocks than through common stocks. Because the price of preferred stocks is related to interest rates and not to earnings, they're protected from big swings in the market. That's a good thing when the market takes a turn for the worse, but it's a bad thing when the market surges.

As a long-term investor, you want to build your wealth primarily from an appreciation of assets (i.e. the rising value of your common stocks). A Class A company might give you a 5% return on preferred stocks — nothing to scoff at — but that won't give you enough to put a down payment on a home. That being said, preferred stocks do have a place in your portfolio.

Let's say you just received your year-end bonus. You want to use it to buy a new car, but your old jalopy still has a few years of life in it. Where should you invest your bonus until your wife says she's tired of taking that junk heap to the repair shop? If you put your money in a savings or checking account, you'll earn a negligible interest rate that gets swallowed up by the rate of inflation. Here's where preferred stocks come to the rescue. Preferred stocks are an ideal place to earn a reasonable dividend for 1-2 years. They pay pretty good interest, and the funds aren't locked up for a long period of time. Just remember to buy preferred stocks through a discount brokerage if you're looking for a short-term investment. The commissions of a full-service brokerage may eat up the dividends you get from the investment.

The Bullet Points of Preferred Stocks

- Preferred stocks are a good asset for your investment portfolio, as they tend to be less volatile than common stocks. They also guarantee dividend payments on fixed dates.

- The limitations of preferred stocks are that they're only offered by select companies, and they're unlikely to turn large profits for the investor.

- Use preferred stocks as a place to park your money for 1-2 years until you need cash.

- Buy preferred stocks through a discount brokerage to prevent buying and selling fees from eating up the dividend.

- Use preferred stocks to diversify your tax-deferred retirement account.

- Only buy cumulative preferred stocks! Doing so will give you the chance of receiving back-pay for companies that eliminate and later restore dividends.

- Buy convertible preferred stocks only if you really believe in the company and think you may want to convert your preferred shares into common shares. Remember — convertible preferred shares typically yield lower dividends.

Master Limited Partnerships (MLPs): Masters of the Dividend

If you're the type of investor who believes in a dividend-heavy strategy, or if you're seeking a low-risk investment that pays a respectable yearly return, check out Master Limited Partnerships. As the name implies, a Master Limited Partnership (MLP) is a partnership — not a corporation or a public company. That means that when you invest in an MLP, you become a unitholder — not a shareholder as you do when you buy a stock. This distinction doesn't have a significant impact on you; it simply means that you aren't invited to annual meetings and you don't have any voting power.

Many MLPs are midstream companies in the energy industry that are responsible for transporting resources from their source to refineries. The strength of MLPs is that they pay a much higher dividend than other investments. Technically speaking, MLPs pay a distribution to unitholders, but you can think of this income as a dividend.

Why are MLP dividends higher than those from other types of investments? It all comes down to taxes. Perhaps you'll recall that common stock dividends are taxed twice: once when the company pays income tax; and again when you receive the dividend. The money available for dividends is therefore reduced because the money has been taxed before distribution. MLPs avoid this double-tax rule by avoiding the first corporate tax. You still have to pay tax on the dividend when you receive it, but eliminating the first slash can be significant. You might ask why

MLPs do not have to pay corporate tax. The reason is that by law, they must distribute about 80% of their earnings to unitholders.

Let's look at an example. Assume that a corporation and an MLP each have $100 available to distribute as a dividend. Each entity has 10 shareholders/unitholders, and the corporate tax is 20%:

Corporation:

- The corporation pays a 20% tax on the $100, leaving $80 for distribution.
- That sum is divided amongst the 10 shareholders, resulting in $8/person

MLP:

- The partnership doesn't have to pay tax on the $100.
- The full $100 is divided amongst the 10 shareholders, resulting in $10/person

There you have it; MLPs consistently provide higher dividends than corporations. I've owned the MLP Enterprise Products Partners (EPD) for many years. At the time of this writing, EPD pays a healthy dividend of 6.72%, and it has raised its dividend every quarter for the past 8 years.

For the most part, MLPs are a relatively safe way to receive steady dividend income. That being said, MLPs are like all investments; they carry a level of risk. In 2014, I bought the MLP Plains All American Pipeline (PAA) for $53.54/unit. At the time, PAA had a very solid balance sheet. However in 2015, one of PAA's pipelines ruptured, causing a massive oil spill. PAA was held responsible, and the MLP plummeted and never recovered. I ultimately sold my shares for $25.19, and it has since dropped to $23.10.

You can reduce the risk of owning one MLP by buying an ETF that includes a variety of MLPs. This might sound good in theory, but I don't suggest it because MLP ETFs are often structured as corporations — not partnerships. That means that they pay tax on income prior to distribution, which reduces the high dividend advantages of MLPs.

MLPs are listed on the stock exchanges, which means that you can buy and sell them just as you would a stock. Comparable brokerage commissions apply on all MLP transactions. If you invest in an MLP, you will receive a notoriously complicated form called the K1 at the end of each year. MLPs use this document to report income in the same way that corporations use a 1099. Save your K1 forms; your accountant will need them to prepare your tax return.

The Bullet Points of MLPs

- An MLP is a partnership and not a corporation.

- Many MLPs are midstream companies in the business of transporting oil and gas. Therefore, the unit price of an MLP usually follows the demand for oil and gas.

- When you buy into a MLP, you buy units and you become a

unit-holder. Unit-holders have no input in the running of the business.

- MLPs distribute income to unitholders as dividends, which tend to be higher for tax reasons.

- Units are bought and sold on the stock exchanges just like a stock, and you pay the same commission as when buying a stock.

- The MLP will send you a K1 at the end of the year showing the distributions you received. Give these to your accountant for preparation of your taxes.

THE VALUE OF FIXED INCOME SECURITIES

Last chapter, we covered three types of investments that can be incorporated into your portfolio to minimize risk. But you might have noticed that mutual funds, preferred stocks, and MLPs still pose an element of risk. After all, their ability to generate income is tied to the performance of individual companies. In this chapter, I want to introduce you to even safer investment types. Everything discussed in the following pages can be classified as fixed income: stable securities pay interest to the investor on a consistent schedule. Our discussion will cover three types of fixed income securities:

- Bonds
- United States Treasuries
- Certificates of Deposit (CDs)

Bonds: The Ultimate IOUs

Years and years ago, I had an acquaintance who liked to bet on horse races. One day, he told me that he was in trouble; he'd placed an ambitious bet with a crooked bookie, and the horse had lost. Owing the bookies wasn't a good thing; they were criminals who took illegal bets on races on the streets. With nowhere else to go, my acquaintance asked if I'd be willing to loan him some money.

"I'll pay it back in full," he said.

"You'll pay it back with interest," I responded.

"Sure," he said, "call it an IOU." We set a date by which he had to pay me back with the money he earned from his job. If he got a bonus, he'd pay it back earlier.

This IOU operated the same exact way as a bond...the only difference is that bonds aren't sold by individuals. Rather, bonds are sold by corporations or municipalities like states, cities, and counties. They can also originate from entities that have a special relationship with a municipality — this includes school districts, toll roads, and water supply companies, among others. Essentially, bonds are sold by any entity that would put you on hold for an inordinate amount of time when calling to complain about service.

Just as my acquaintance asked for money when he needed to pay off his bookie, bonds originate when a company needs cash for a certain project. When you buy a bond, you're loaning money to the issuer of the bond. In exchange, the issuer agrees to pay you interest payments, which are paid in fixed installments on a firm schedule. These interest payments will keep coming in for the full term of the bond, at which the bond 'reaches maturity,' or until the bond is 'called.' But interest payments aren't an investor's only income from a bond. Once the bond reaches maturity, you'll receive a principal, which is the face value of the bond. The principal is not necessarily what you pay for the bond; the difference will be explained shortly.

For example, let's say that you buy 5 bonds with a face value of $1,000 each, paying 6% interest. Here's a breakdown of all the amounts you would receive through the lifetime of the bond.

Annual Interest Payments:

.06 (Annual Interest Rate) x 5,000 (Total Face Value) = **$300 (Paid Each Year)**

Principal:

5 (Number of Bonds Purchased) x $1,000 (Face Value of Each Bond) = **$5,000**

Because brokerages often mark up the price of the bond (discussed later in this chapter), the face value is often lower than what you pay for the bond upfront. Remember that the principal is the face value — not the amount that you bought the bond for.

Bonds are typically long-term investments, with maturity terms of up to thirty years. After maturity, the bond is completed and you won't receive any more interest payments. It's important to note that interest payments are different from dividends; interest is a fixed amount payable on a schedule, whereas a dividend can be adjusted at the discretion of the issuing company.

Some bonds, especially those issued by municipalities, have call provisions. These allow the issuer of the bond to buy back the bond after a set date prior to maturity, usually at the face amount of the bond but occasionally at a premium. If a company decides to use its call provision, the bond is rendered complete and you'll stop receiving your interest payments. You should note that bonds with call provisions tend to have a slightly higher interest rate.

How to buy a bond

Just like stocks, you buy bonds through brokerages. They are sold in lots of $1,000, which means that you have to buy bonds in increments of $1,000, $2,000, $3,000 — so on and so forth.

When the issuer of the bond needs to raise capital for a project, it sells the bond to a brokerage house. That brokerage becomes known as the underwriter, as it sells the bond to the general public after marking up the price to make a profit. This markup includes the fee to buy the bond, which means you don't pay a commission to purchase a bond.

It follows that you can get good or bad deals on a bond, depending on the markup assigned by the underwriter. Luckily, you can assess this markup by comparing the selling price to par, the face value of a bond. Here's the trick: bonds are always quoted based on a scale of 100, 100 being par. Take a look at the following bond details as an example:

Bond A:

Face Value: $1,000
Selling Price: $1,000
100.0 Rating (At Par)

This means that the underwriter bought the bond for less than $1,000 and is selling it at par; that is, $1,000. This rarely happens in the real world; here's a more realistic example:

Bond B:

Face Value: $1,000
Selling Price: $1,150
115.0 Rating

Bottom line — look for bonds with ratings as close to 100 as possible!

All bonds are identified by a CUSIP number, which is like a social security number for the bond. On the off-chance that you're a sucker for acronyms, CUSIP stands for "Committee on Uniform Securities Identification Procedures." Looking at a CUSIP number can help you identify bonds being sold at different interest rates, call provisions, and maturity dates.

Because bonds aren't available on stock exchanges, brokerages can only sell the bonds that they have in their inventory. That means that the availability of bonds may vary from brokerage to brokerage. Also, individual investors like you and me tend to pay more for bonds than institutional investors such as pension funds and mutual funds. This is because institutional investors do far more business with brokerages than the individual.

An Example

Let's look at an example to clarify what we know about bonds. Assume that a brokerage offers a 30-year 5% bond callable in 10 years for 115.0. Let's dissect that:

Bond Term: 30 Years
Annual Interest Rate: 5%
Call Provision: 10 Years
Markup Rating: 115.0

This means that you're paying $1,150 for each $1,000 lot (the brokerage is pocketing $150 per lot). Let's say that you bite on this bond and purchase 25 bonds. Here's how much you would be paying:

25 x $1,150 =
$28,750

Let's move onto your annual interest payments:

.05 (Interest Rate) x $25,000 (Face value of your bond purchase) =
$1,250

Even though this bond has a call provision of 10 years, let's say that the issuer of the bond chooses to not exercise it. In that case, the bond will remain active for its full term of 30 years. At maturity, you'll receive a principal of $25,000, the face value of your initial purchase. That's the big check that you've been waiting for, though note that it's the face value of your initial purchase — not the $28,750 that you paid for the bond. With all of that in mind, let's calculate how much you made on this bond:

Total Interest Payments:

$1,250 (Annual Interest Payment) x 30 (Bond Term) =
$37,500

Total Received:

$37,500 (Total Interest Payment) + $25,000 (Face Value Payment) =
$62,500

Total Profit:

$62,500 (Total Received) - $28,750 (Initial Investment) =
$33,750

No one should scoff at $33,750. That being said, investing in common stocks has the potential of making you a lot more money over a 30-year period. The attractive thing about bonds is how safe they are.

As I noted earlier, if a bond has a call provision, it may be called by its issuer. You can imagine that your total profit would be considerably lower if this bond were to be called before reaching maturity. While you'd receive your face value payment, you'd be missing out on years of interest payments.

Bonds & Taxes

Unfortunately, taxes are always something to worry about. All corporate bonds are subject to local, state, and federal tax. However, most municipal bonds are tax-exempt; we'll limit our discussion to tax-free municipal bonds because they make up the majority. Here's the catch in investing in tax-free bonds: in order for interest payments to be tax-free, the bond must invest in the state where the buyer lives. For example, if you're a resident of California like I am, you should only buy bonds issued by California. Buying a bond from Arizona would defeat the purpose of buying a municipal bond, as you would have to pay taxes on interest payments.

Bond Funds

Rather than buying individual bonds, you can buy professionally-managed bond funds, which include a bundle of bonds with varying maturities, risk levels, and issuers. Bond funds can be purchased through brokerages like regular bonds. You can think of bond funds like mutual funds or ETFs — they offer a way for you to invest in bonds without hedging your bets on a single bond. Another benefit of bond funds is that they allow you to invest in bonds for less than $1,000 per lot. Rather than having to buy an entire bond, you can contribute a dollar amount to a bond fund and receive a portion of a given bond. This can be a great asset to investors who are on a budget and don't have thousands of dollars to fling at different bonds.

How to evaluate a bond

Now that we know how bonds work, how can we distinguish between good and bad ones? I suggest looking at the following metrics:

- **Yield to Maturity (YTM) aka Yield to Par** — for bonds that reach maturity

- **Yield to Call (YTC) aka Yield to Worst** — for bonds
  that are called before maturity
- **Bond Credit Ratings**

Let's start with Yield to Maturity (YTM). YTM, expressed as an annual percent, is a rate that anticipates the total return on a bond if it's held to maturity. YTM takes several factors into account such as the term of the bond, the interest rate, and the difference between the principal and what you paid for the bond. Yield to Call (YTC) is the same as YTM, except it's adjusted for bonds that are called before maturity. It follows that YTC is consistently lower than YTM because it assumes you're missing out on interest payments.

Both YTM and YTC have a somewhat intricate calculation, but any bond listing will provide these figures for you. Remember how for closed mutual funds, we had to compare the NAV/share to the price per share in order to determine whether the fund was valuable? The same thing goes for YTM and YTC with bonds. In order to determine what a good YTM or YTC is, we need to compare it to inflation, specifically the Consumer Price Index (CPI). I recommend that a bond's YTM should be at least 3% higher than the CPI; in the year 2019, that means around 5%.

Another way to evaluate the worth of a bond is to look at the bond credit rating of the issuer. A high rating means that the issuer is likely to pay annual interest payments and the principal at the time of maturity. A low rating indicates a higher probability of the issuer defaulting on the bond. The major rating agencies evaluate investment grade bonds from AAA (triple A) to BBB- (triple B minus). Bonds rated less than BBB- are considered junk.

While these ratings are worth reviewing, we can't overly rely too much on them. The rating agencies have a conflict of interest, as they are commonly paid by the entities being rated. During the financial crisis of 2007-2008, these agencies gave approval ratings to bonds that should have been rated as junk. With that said, stick to investment grade bonds and forget those with junk ratings.

Bond Strategy

If you decide to incorporate bonds into your portfolio, consider the following suggestions. These strategies will ensure that you turn a healthy profit from your bonds.

1. Hold your bond until it is called or reaches maturity.

If you find yourself needing cash before your bond's maturity date, you can sell a bond back to a brokerage house prior to its maturity date. Avoid doing this at all costs. The brokerage will bail you out, but they'll pay far less than what the bond is worth. Selling before maturity is a surefire way to lose money on a bond.

2. Choose bonds with relatively short maturity terms.

It's safer to buy bonds with short maturity terms (somewhere between 5 and 10 years) because it's impossible to predict future interest rates. Bond prices tend to move inversely to interest rates. That means that if interest rates spike, the price of your bond could drop significantly.

In addition, bonds tend to appreciate in value as they approach maturity. That means you may find yourself being tempted to sell your bond for an increased price as it approaches maturity, but don't. The amount that you would be receiving for your bond would not adequately compensate for the loss of your interest payments.

3. If you're seeking a risk-averse bond, consider buying General Obligation Bonds issued by a State.

Some of the safest bonds that you can buy are called General Obligation Bonds (GO Bonds). GO bonds are a type of municipal bond that have strong backing by a community and are unlikely to go under. The most secure type of GO bonds, however, are those issued by a state as opposed to a city or a county. This is because cities and counties can technically go bankrupt, while states cannot.

4. 'Ladder' your portfolio with bonds that have different maturities.

By purchasing bonds with varying maturity rates, you can protect yourself against fluctuating interest rates. This is an important way to diversify your bond holdings. I recommend holding bonds with maturities at 1, 3, 5, 7, and 10 years. Let's say you buy a 10-year bond. In 3 years, it will become a 7-year bond. At that time, you should look for another 10-year bond. In 2 more years, the initial 10-year bond will be a 5-year bond, and the second 10-year bond will be an 8-year bond, and so on.

5. Consider hiring a bond specialist to purchase bonds and bond funds.

Because there isn't a published market for bonds like there is for stocks, I've found that bond specialists are worth their fees. Not only are good specialists aware of the numerous bonds available, they can leverage better prices than the individual can.

The Bullet Points of Bonds

- Bonds are a safe, fixed income security that allows you to loan money to an issuing entity in exchange for interest payments.

- Look at the bond's markup rating. Remember that you're shooting towards 'par,' which is 100.0. The higher the rating, the worse your yield.

- Determine whether the bond is taxable or tax-exempt. If it happens to be tax-exempt, evaluate the interest rate. Many tax-exempt bonds have very low interest rates and can be less profitable than taxable bonds that have higher interest payments.

- Compare a bond's Yield to Maturity (YTM) and Yield to Call (YTC) to the Consumer Price Index to determine whether it's a good bond to buy. The YTM should be at least 3% higher than the CPI. You can expect the YTC to be lower than the YTM because it assumes that you're missing out on interest payments

- Take a look at the bond's credit rating to determine the likelihood of the issuer defaulting on the bond.

- When buying a tax-exempt municipal bond, be sure that it's issued in the state where you live to get the full benefit of the tax exemption.

- When buying municipal bonds, consider buying General Obligation Bonds (GOs) backed by a state.

- Hold your bonds until they are called, or until they reach maturity.

- Implement a 'laddering' strategy so that you have bonds with varying maturity terms.

- Consider hiring a bond specialist if you want to incorporate bonds into your portfolio.

/

United States Treasuries — the Unicorn Investment?

What if I told you that there was a type of investment that had all of the following benefits?

- You can't lose the money that you invest
- You're guaranteed to receive interest payments
- The interest that you earn is exempt from local and state taxes
- You don't have to pay a commission to make the investment

Sounds like the unicorn that we've all been looking for, right? Well, you can actually get all of these features by investing in United States Treasuries, loans to our country's government. When you buy a Treasury, you're guaranteed two sources of income: 1) your interest payments on the dates specified; and 2) the return of the principal at the maturity date. Aside from treasuries, there is no other investment that offers such a complete guarantee.

Think about all of the class A investments that I discussed in Chapter 4 that went belly up. Pacific Gas and Electric — bankruptcy; Bear Stearns — bankruptcy; FannieMae and Freddie Mac — bankruptcy. Unfortunately, bankruptcy happens far more often than one might hope. Investing in treasuries allows the investor to escape risk because the country cannot declare bankruptcy. In other words, a government will never default on its financial obligations to you — the investor — if you decide to purchase a treasury. Your investment — that is, your interest payments and your principal — is 100% guaranteed by the government. What's the downside to that? With this level of security, treasuries pay less interest than other investments with similar maturity terms.

The interest received from U.S Treasuries is exempt from state and local taxes but subject to federal tax. This can be a significant benefit to those who live in states like California that impose high state and local taxes. Now that we know that treasuries are, let me outline what kind of treasuries are available for purchase. The government offers a variety of investments, but there are three that are appropriate for the individual investor.

United States Bills

United States Bills reach maturity anywhere from 4 weeks to 1 year, and they are sold in $100 increments. Bills do not pay interest in the classic sense of receiving a payment at certain intervals. Instead, the earned interest is determined by the difference between the face amount of the bill on the maturity date and the amount you paid for the bill. Your interest is collected in one lump on the maturity date — not in installments as in other types of investments.

For example, if you bought a $100 bill and paid $95, you would receive $100 at maturity. The difference of $5 would be your interest.

United States Notes

United States Notes have maturity terms ranging from 1 to 10 years. Just like bills, notes are sold in increments of $100. You can buy notes with two types of interest rates — floating or fixed. Opt for the latter! The interest that you receive with floating rates changes based on parameters that make them unpredictable. When you buy a note with a fixed interest rate, you know exactly how much money your investment will earn. Notes pay interest twice per year.

Treasury Inflation Protected Securities (TIPS)

Treasury Inflation Protected Securities (TIPS), which have maturities of 5, 10, and 30 years, are a type of treasury that serve as a hedge against inflation. The interest collected from TIPS are determined by two things: 1) a fixed coupon rate; and 2) a floating principal. The principal changes with respect to the Consumer Price Index (CPI). Remember — the CPI is essentially the rate of inflation.

When the CPI moves up, the principal of the TIPS increases as well. Conversely, when the CPI drops, the principal of the TIPS will drop in suit. You can find your interest payments by multiplying the fixed coupon rate by the floating principal. Interest is paid every six months, and the principal is adjusted prior to the following interest payment date. Let's look at an example:

TIPS A:

Principal: $100
Coupon Rate: 3%

Let's calculate your interest payment, which you would collect every 6 months:

100 (Principal) x .03 (Coupon Rate) =
$3 (Annual Interest)

$3 / 2 (Number of payments/year) =
$1.50

Now, let's say that the CPI moves up, driving the principal to $110. Then, your interest would shift to the following:

110 (Principal) x .03 (Coupon Rate) =
$3.30 (Annual Interest)

$3.30 / 2 (Number of payments/year) =
$1.65

If the CPI moves down, dropping the principal to $90, you'd receive the following:

90 (Principal) x .03 (Coupon Rate) =
$2.70 (Annual Interest)

$2.70 / 2 (Number of payments/year) =
$1.35

These adjusted interest rates are put in place to guard the investor against the tides of inflation.

How to Buy a Treasury

You can buy treasuries without having to pay a commission to the United States Treasury Department. Any U.S. citizen over the age of 18 can open an account with the Treasury

Department. The Treasury Department holds an auction each week for notes, bills, bonds, and TIPS. When you place an order, you can specify the type and amount of treasury that you want to buy; then, you must accept whatever rate is determined by the auction. Detailed information on how to handle transactions through the Treasury Department can be found on the "TreasuryDirect" website.

You can also buy treasuries through your brokerage, but make sure that yours doesn't charge a commission. If your brokerage allows you to buy commission-free treasuries, I suggest going that way; it's simpler and your investments are all in one place.

The Bullet Points of United States Treasuries

- Treasuries are a risk-averse investment that guarantees interest payments and your principal investment.

- While treasuries are safe, they should not be the focus of a young investor's portfolio. They should be incorporated into established portfolios to minimize risk.

- Treasuries can be purchased online from the Treasury Department or through a standard brokerage.

- United States Bills have relatively short maturity terms (~1 month - 1 year). Interest is paid when the bill expires.

- United States Notes have longer maturity terms (~1 year - 10 years). Interest is paid twice per year.

- Treasury Inflation Protected Securities (TIPS) have maturity terms of 5, 10, and 30 years. TISP protect you from inflation by having a floating principal that mirrors the CPI.

- Treasuries are worth considering if you fear an economic recession may be coming, you live in a high taxation state such as California, or the CPI rises rapidly and drives inflation to high levels.

/

Certificates of Deposit (CDs): Investments for the Short-Timer

The Armed Forces have a term for draftees who are up for discharge: short-timers. These men and women are eager to get home to their families, which means they avoid hazardous duties that might hold up their discharge. In essence, they seek safety.

You may find yourself in a similar boat in your investing career. Despite your long-term strategy, there will be times when you need to make a short-term investment. Perhaps you know that you're going to have to make a big purchase within 2 years. You don't have to buy anything in the present, and keeping your money in a savings account won't earn you any interest. Certificates of Deposit (CDs) are a great option for parking your money for a short period of time. Not only are CDs risk-free and guaranteed by the FDIC for up to $250,000, they tend to have strong interest rates. In fact, CDs almost invariably outperform treasuries when it comes to interest.

CDs act like a bank savings account with one exception: you must agree to leave your money with the bank until the CD expires. In other words, you don't have the flexibility to access the money invested in a CD. Some CDs offer a provision that allows for early withdrawal, which is accompanied by a stiff penalty fee. But if you decide to invest in a CD, plan to leave the money invested until the CD expires. Unless you buy a CD with funds from your retirement account (we'll discuss these in the next chapter), the interest earned from CDs is taxed as ordinary income.

How to buy a CD

When it comes to buying, CDs are like bonds — they're sold by brokerage houses. The CD rate quoted by your brokerage includes the brokerage's commission, so there aren't any additional fees. Before you buy a CD, I recommend taking the following steps:

- Determine how long you want the CD to run. The maturity dates of CDs range from 4 weeks to over 2 years, but they work best as a short-term investment. I wouldn't buy a CD with a maturity of over 2 years; there are better investments for the long term (stocks, ETFs, index funds).
- Ask your brokerage for a list of CDs that suit your

maturity term. Your brokerage should provide a number of options from a slew of different banks.

- Choose the CD that pays the highest interest. You'll notice that interest rates vary from bank to bank; the highest one will produce the best return for you. Don't be concerned if you haven't heard of the bank in question; just be sure that it's FDIC-insured.

Once you've decided on a CD, your brokerage can buy it for you immediately. Many banks stipulate an investment minimum of $100 for CDs, though some banks might have higher minimums.

The Bullet Points of CDs

- CDs are a good place to invest money for the short-term — that is, anywhere from 4 weeks to 2 years.

- CDs should be bought from FDIC-insured banks.

- Plan to leave your money in the CD until the CD matures, as early removal will cost you dearly.

- CDs tend to generate higher interest rates than U.S. treasuries.

There you have it — we've made it through all the fixed income securities that can offset the risks of investing in common stocks. While bonds, treasuries, and CDs all have a place in one's investment portfolio, don't make them the benchmark of your portfolio when you're just starting out. All of these options are extremely risk-averse, which means that they have low ceilings for producing wealth. Only start implementing fixed-income securities once you've become an established investor.

TAXES & ACCOUNTS: YOUR BURDEN & YOUR BUCKETS

Baseball, which has come to be known as America's pastime, is an outlier in the world of athletics. While other sports like basketball and football rely on raw talent, baseball is a game of strategy. Aside from the abilities of his players, the manager of a baseball team has to consider pitch count, batting lineups, ballpark dimensions, and a slew of other components that play a role in the outcome of the game. Being an investor is much like being the manager of a baseball team. Knowing how to throw and hit is just part of the battle; you need to know how to play the game.

This chapter covers some of those game components; namely, the impact of taxes and accounts. Let's get started.

You Must Pay The Piper: The Factor of Taxes

There's an old story that describes a town overrun with rats. One day, a man comes along and says that if the townspeople pay him a fee, he can get rid of the vermin. The town readily agrees and watches the man start to play his magical pipe. The rats follow his music, marching into a nearby creek where they drown. When the piper returns to the town to collect his fee, the townspeople refuse to pay. The piper responds that if he doesn't get his money, he'll play his magical pipe and the children will follow him into the creek.

It suffices to say that if you don't pay the piper, bad things will happen. In the world of investing, the piper equates to taxes. When you open an investment account, you agree to pay income tax on your profits. Now, there are two main types of income tax: federal and state. Every American citizen is obligated to pay federal income tax, and 41 states also impose state income tax. I'll confine our discussion to Federal Tax because it plays a significant role in your investment behavior.

The amount of tax that the individual must pay is determined by tax brackets set in place by the government. These brackets mandate a certain percentage of your income to be paid as tax. Tax brackets are bound to change with shifts in the government, but one trend remains constant: the more money you make, the higher your tax bracket will be. Why isn't everyone taxed at the same rate, you might ask? Well, if the tax rate was constant — say at 30% for all income levels

— a person making a $30,000 yearly salary would be taking home $21,000. That's next to nothing by the standards of modern costs of living. On the other hand, a person making $3 million would be taking home $2.1 million, a very tidy amount. Uncle Sam recognizes that wealthy people can handle giving up more of their wages to the government, while lower-income people can ill-afford to pay high taxes. All of this leads to our tax brackets, where the rich pay a greater percent of their income and the less fortunate pay a lower percent.

If you're just starting out or you're only working part-time, there's a minimum income below which you don't have to file a federal tax form. The threshold for not filing depends on a variety of factors including income, marital status, and age. The threshold in 2018 for an unmarried person less than 65 was $12,000. However, the government changes its rules frequently; if you don't have much income, check with your accountant to determine if you need to file federal income taxes.

Since your tax rate is determined by your income, we need to have a clear understanding of what 'income' really is. Income isn't just the amount that you receive from your employer or what you earn if self-employed; it relates to any profit received, with the exception of gifts. In other words, any money received when you sell a stock for a profit (as well as any interest or dividends) is classified as income, which is then subject to the Federal Income Tax.

All of this is to say that by the annual tax deadline, April

15th, you must report your gains and losses, dividends, and interest payments to Uncle Sam, the Internal Revenue Service (IRS), and the state in which you live. If this sounds like a major pain, that's because it is! Luckily, accountants specialize in helping you prepare tax returns, and your brokerage house keeps records and notifies the IRS of all sales, dividends, and interest payments. At the end of the year, companies and municipalities that paid a dividend or interest will send you a form — either the '1099' or the 'K1' — which will show the dividend or interest payment that you received. You must keep these records for your accountant who will prepare your tax return.

Tax Rates: Short-Term vs Long-Term Investments

While income from your salary and income from your investments are both subject to federal tax, they're taxed at different rates. Tax rates on investments are largely determined by how long you've held the investment. Profits from your investments are classified into two categories: "short-term" gains and "long-term" gains. Short-term profits correspond to stocks held for less than 1 year and are taxed at a higher rate, which is known as the ordinary rate. The ordinary rate is about the same as tax on salary income. Long-term profits are collected on stocks held for more than 1 year and are taxed at a considerably lower rate, called the capital gains rate. As of 2019, the maximum short-term federal tax rate is 37% while the maximum long-term rate is 20%. This is yet another reason why long-term investing is an advantageous strategy; it saves you money on taxes.

At some point in your career, you're bound to sell a stock for less money than you paid for it. Even though you receive money in your account when you sell for a loss, you don't have to pay taxes on this amount because it isn't income. In fact, you may be able to deduct these losses from your tax payments. The rules about gains and losses are beyond the scope of this book — let's leave that to your accountant.

Keeping Your Accounts

So far, we've discussed how to make money in the stock market, but we haven't dipped our toe into the ocean of how to keep your accounts. Eventually, you're going to become an accountant — not for yourself, but for your own funds. At first glance, it might seem like accounts don't matter all that much. After all, money is money — it shouldn't matter what box you put it in. Unfortunately, that mindset isn't accurate. Allocating where you put your money will have a significant impact on your wealth, largely because of tax purposes.

Eventually, you should have four accounts — two for everyday living, and two for investments:

- **Checking account** — for everyday living
- **Savings account** — for everyday living
- **Taxable investment account** — for investments
- **Retirement investment account** — for investments

Let's break these down...

Your Everyday Accounts: Checking & Savings

Checking and savings accounts are used for the expenses of everyday life. Both of these accounts should be set up with the same bank so that it's easy to transfer money from one to the other. Today, it's easier than ever to manage your accounts with online banking. One of the cardinal traits of checking and savings accounts is that they're FDIC-insured. To reiterate, that means that the funds placed in these accounts is 100% secure for up to $250,000. Even if your financial institution goes belly-up, the government will return that money to you.

One of the most common account-related mistakes is placing either too little or too much money in these everyday accounts. On one hand, you need to allocate enough money to cover your expenses. But on the other, setting aside too much money in these accounts will limit the amount of money for your investment accounts. Remember that your everyday accounts pay very little interest. In fact, you can pretty much count on the interest rates being below the Consumer Price Index (CPI), the rate of inflation. That means that every dollar placed in an everyday account is depreciating over time.

Deciding how much money to put into your everyday accounts is a personal decision. That being said, I recommend splitting about six months of your expenses between your checking and savings accounts. You want to have enough money to cover any large, unexpected bills that could fall on your shoulders at a moment's notice. Having a six-month nest egg is a reasonable amount that you can dip into, should life throw you a curveball.

Ultimately, we should think of checking and savings accounts as our financial safety net. Because the funds in these accounts are risk-free, we can rely on them if we encounter costly, unanticipated events. That being said, we should avoid putting too much money in these accounts because they won't grow our wealth. Perhaps you've heard the phrase "money makes more money" — unfortunately, that doesn't apply to the dollars in checking and savings accounts.

Checking Accounts

Your checking account is the first account that you need. This is the bucket that contains your spending money. A checking account is like a reservoir, but instead of water, money flows in with deposits and out with checks or debit charges. When you open a checking account with a bank, you'll receive a debit card, which uses the funds from your checking account. A quick warning on debit cards: since they allow money to be withdrawn directly from your account, they're vulnerable to hacking schemes. Debit cards should only be used to deposit and withdraw money from an ATM. A credit card should be used to make purchases.

Checking accounts get their name from physical checks, but

the world is changing; checks are becoming less and less common. Whether you use your debit card or checks, I'm going to lean on you to do something tedious but important; you must review your bank's checking account statement as soon as it's released. Banks will send monthly statements that show every purchase, deposit, and withdrawal that has occurred over the course of a given month. It's key to make sure that the account statement matches what you've actually spent that month. Not only does this ensure that no fraud is being committed, it will make you aware of how much you're spending each month. Swiping a plastic card doesn't feel like spending money, but it's important to realize how quickly your account can be diminished if you aren't careful about budgeting.

It's important to keep more money in your checking account than needed. Not only is the event of a debit charge or check "bouncing" embarrassing, it can result in stiff penalty costs from your bank.

Savings Accounts

Your bank will set you up with a savings account at the same time that you get your checking account. Think of your savings account as an overflow account when you have more money than you need for your checking account. You don't want to leave a large amount in your checking account because those funds earn negligible interest. Savings accounts are used for parking spare cash in a place that's readily accessible and earns better interest than a checking account.

/

Investing Accounts: Taxable and Tax-Deferred Retirement

All of your investments will fall into either a Taxable or Tax-Deferred Retirement account. These are commonly referred to as your portfolio, as they include your flock of investments. I recommend setting up your investment accounts with the same financial institution with which you have your checking and savings account. Doing so makes it easy for you to move money from one account to another. For instance, your employer will probably automatically deposit your paychecks into your checking account. If you're exhibiting a sound budgeting strategy, you'll frequently want to transfer funds from your checking account to one of your investing accounts.

Taxable Investment Accounts

Anyone can open a taxable investment account. In this type of account, the money invested has already been taxed as income, and the government gives you no tax break. That's unfortunate — you have to pay appropriate tax on interest, dividends, and any gains when the securities are sold. That being said, taxable investment accounts do not have any restrictions on deposits or withdrawals. You can invest as much or as little as you want, and your money isn't locked up for a period of time.

Tax-Deferred Retirement Investment Accounts

Thinking about retirement at this stage may seem silly, but trust me: it creeps up on you. When you start to make money, you should open up a retirement account to set aside funds for the inevitable day that you stop working. This might sound like we're veering off-course from investing, but bear with me: this stuff matters.

Retirement accounts are defined by the fact that the funds are locked up until the age of retirement, which is 59½. You should plan on not needing the money contributed to a retirement account until you reach that age. If catastrophe strikes and you need to access the funds, you can do so by paying a hefty penalty. Once you turn 59½, you can start withdrawing money from your retirement accounts without penalty. Once you turn 72, you must begin to withdraw your money; in fact, there's a minimum amount that you must withdraw each year. This is called a Required Minimum Distribution (RMD), but you won't have to worry about that for several decades.

Individual Retirement Accounts (IRAs): Traditional vs Roth

Most companies set up their employees with a 401 K account, a retirement account that's managed by financial experts to build wealth over time. But in addition to that, I suggest opening up an Individual Retirement Account (IRA) as soon as possible. Now, there are two types of retirement plans: Traditional IRAs, which are taxed when you take the money out; and Roth IRAs, which are taxed up-front. Let's discuss which one is right for you.

In a Traditional IRA, your contributions to the fund are not taxed. If you want to throw in $1,000, that full $1,000 gets added to the account; you don't have to pay any tax to the government up-front. However, there is no free lunch with the government. At the time of retirement, the money that you withdraw will be taxed as ordinary income, regardless of how long that money has been invested.

Roth IRAs work in the reverse. The money that you invest into a Roth is taxed up-front. However, you avoid paying taxes when you withdraw the money at the time of retirement. For this reason, we can refer to the Roth IRA as a tax-deferred retirement account. An added caveat to Roth IRAs; there's a limit to how much you can contribute each year. At the time of this writing, you can max out a Roth IRA at $6,000 annually, assuming you're making less than $137,000 each year. Once again, these rules are subject to change, so best to consult your accountant.

Let me demonstrate by way of example. Assume that in a given year, we have the following specifications:

- Annual Income: $50,000
- Tax Rate: 10%
- IRA Investment: $5,000

In a Traditional IRA, your $5,000 contribution to the IRA is exempt from taxes. That means that your 10% tax only applies to $45,000 of your income ($50,000 - $5,000). Here's how you would find your taxes owed and your net income.

Traditional IRA:

$45,000 (Taxable Income) x 0.1 (Tax Rate) =
$4,500 (Taxes Owed)

$50,000 (Annual Income) - $4,500 (Taxes Owed) =
$45,500 (Net Income)

In a Roth IRA, you have to pay tax on the whole $50,000, even though $5,000 is going into your retirement account. Let's do the same math and see what happens.

Roth IRA:

$50,000 (Taxable Income) x 0.1 (Tax Rate) =
$5,000 (Taxes Owed)

$50,000 (Annual Income) - $5,000 (Taxes Owed) =
$45,000 (Net Income)

At first glance, the Traditional seems more favorable than the Roth. After all, you're getting $500 less with the Roth than you would with the Traditional. But that's not the case; once you withdraw funds from your Traditional IRA, you're going to have a tax liability. With the Roth, you've already paid the tax associated with the funds in your account.

This discussion of Traditional vs Roth IRAs boils down to one point. *If you think that you'll be making more money at the time of retirement than you're making now, you should open up a Roth IRA.* The Roth is a much better choice if you can afford a slightly lower take-home pay. Over the years, your Roth IRA will build up lots of money, and being able to withdraw it without paying tax is a huge advantage.

Regardless or the plan you choose, contribute the maximum amount allowed: the tax advantage of a retirement account is a great way to build up income.

Compounding in a Tax-Deferred Retirement Account

The advantage of a tax-deferred retirement account is that you avoid paying taxes on money earned from that account. That means no taxes on dividends and no taxes on interest payments. Eluding these taxes results in an effect called compounding, which we discussed earlier in our section on dividend reinvestment. Compounding works wonders in a tax-deferred account. I'll demonstrate by way of example.

Let's say that you place $100 in a tax-deferred account. Each year, you add $100, and your investment earns 6%. After 20 years, your investment would be worth $4,219, and after 40 years, your investment would be worth $17,433. Not too shabby. The advantages of having a tax-deferred account are obvious; I recommend opening one up as soon as you can.

Now, I'm going to let you on a secret number that can be used in compounding interest: the number is 72. If you divide an interest rate into 72, the answer is the number of years it will take for your money to double. Alternatively, if you divide the number of years into 72, the result is the interest rate required to double your money.

For example, suppose you want to know how many years it will take for $100 to double at 5% interest, compounded annually:

72 / 5 (interest rate) =
14.4 years

Now let's say that you're searching for the interest rate that will allow you investment of $100 to double in 10 years:

72 / 10 (years) =
7.2%

This trick can be tremendously helpful if you want to project the performance of your accounts.

Investment strategies for your Tax-Deferred Retirement Account

We've established that Tax-Deferred Retirement Accounts are the way to go, but that leaves an open question: how should we invest the money from those accounts? Let's talk about which types of investments are best suited for your Roth IRA retirement account. Overall, there are two parameters that come into play:

- In a tax-deferred retirement account, all money
  earned from dividends, interest payments, and profits
  from selling a stock are free of taxation. Any losses
  from selling a stock are not deductible.
- Taxable municipal and corporate bonds pay more
  interest than tax-free bonds.

Given these factors, I recommend pursuing the following
investments for your Tax-Deferred Retirement Account (i.e.,
your Roth IRA):

- Corporate and taxable municipal bonds. These have
  strong interest rates. In a taxable investment account,
  you would have to pay tax on your earnings. But by
  placing these investments in a tax-deferred retirement
  account, you avoid paying taxes.
- Preferred stocks. These usually pay a high dividend,
  around 5%, which can be significant when you aren't
  paying taxes on the earnings. Investing at 5%, your
  money will double in twelve years. If you keep a
  preferred stock in a retirement account for 48 years,
  the amount in the account will double four times.
- Master Limited Partnerships (MLPs). These generate
  high dividends by avoiding tax levies.

On the other hand, you should avoid buying stocks for your
retirement account that pay little or no dividend. Companies
like Amazon, Berkshire Hathaway, and Facebook are strong
investments that you may want to pursue in other areas of

your portfolio, but not for a retirement account. There are two reasons for this: 1) they don't pay high dividends; and 2) they will be subject to higher tax rates — not the more favorable "long-term" rate that you would get in a regular investment account.

A final thought on managing your IRA. Because all investments in a retirement account are taxed at the same rate (there isn't a tax distinction between short-term and long-term investments), don't hesitate to sell a stock quickly if you have a good reason to do so.

/

The Bullet Points

- Use the same financial institution for your checking, savings, investing, and retirement accounts.

- Federal income tax — and sometimes state income tax — are unavoidable expenses that should be factored into your finances.

- Your profits from investments are taxed as income. That being said, gains from long-term investments are taxed at a lower rate than gains from short-term investments.

- Profits from long-term investments are taxed as capital gains, while profits from short-term investments are taxed at an ordinary rate. The ordinary rate is always higher than the capital gains rate.

- Keep every tax-related form in a safe place for your accountant! Losing your 1099 and K1 forms can be a real pain. Your brokerage is obligated to send you your tax forms.

- The first accounts that you'll need are your checking & savings accounts. Use these to handle your day-to-day finances, but avoid hoarding money in them.

- Once you have a substantial nest egg in your checking and savings accounts, start your investment portfolio in a taxable investment account.

- Open up a tax-deferred retirement account — specifically a Roth IRA — as soon as you can! Do your best to max out your Roth IRA every year. That being said, remember that the funds contributed to this account won't be accessible to you until you're at least 59 ½.

- Fill your Tax-Deferred Retirement Account with corporate and taxable municipal bonds, preferred stocks, and MLPs.

- Avoid filling your Tax-Deferred Retirement Account with investments that do not produce interest or dividends.

- Don't buy risky stocks for your Tax-Deferred Retirement account. If they go sour, you can't deduct the loss.

9
SETTING THE TABLE FOR YOUR FUTURE

When I was teaching my kids how to drive, I spent lots of time demonstrating safe driving techniques. But just as important — and perhaps more memorable to them — was when I pointed out what not to do on the road. That's what I intend to do for you now. Let's discuss some high-risk investments that you'll hear about but are not for you.

/

Puts and Calls (Options)

At some point along your investing career, you'll hear about buying and selling puts and calls. What are these all about? *Puts and calls, collectively known as options, are risky investments that should be left to financial professionals.* A call is the right to buy a stock at a predetermined price (the strike price) within a specified time (the exercise date). A put is the exact same thing, except it involves selling the stock at the strike price. These transactions are always accompanied by a premium, which is paid at the time of purchase. All of this business of puts and calls is referred to as option trading because you're essentially buying the option to buy or sell a stock.

If you find this information dense, you've lucked out; I suggest that you don't burden yourself with puts and calls. Option trading is gambling, not investing, and goes against the grain of this book. I tried my hand at selling calls and received a few moderate successes at the expense of a few major sacrifices. When the trades worked out, I generally made about 8-10% in 6-12 months. But on two occasions, selling calls backfired and cost me more than I made on all the calls I ever sold. When you invest in a company that you feel has a good future, stick with it and have faith in your judgment. Don't try to make a few extra dollars by dabbling with puts and calls.

Structured Products

Your broker may offer you an investment called a structured product. There are all kinds of structured products, but the most common are like a short-term bond with contingent interest rates. Structured products often mature in 2 to 3 years and present 2 interest rates: a Guaranteed Rate and a Potential Rate, which I call the kicker. The Guaranteed Rate will always be lower than the going interest rate, and the Potential

Rate will always be higher than the going interest rate. If you buy the structured product, you're hoping that a number of factors will allow the Potential Rate to kick in. Otherwise, you're stuck with the lower Guaranteed Rate. Whether or not the Potential Rate applies is determined by a number of factors such as the price of oil, gold, and rates set by LIBOR (the London Interbank Offered Rate).

I want you to stay away from structured products. They're put together by very smart professional investors and are designed to profit the issuing company, not the individual investor. If you buy a structured product, you're gambling on interest rates or some other financial index. When the time comes when you want to add fixed income securities to your portfolio, stick to the bread and butter ones that were covered in Chapter 7.

Borrowing Money to Buy Stocks

This monster is pretty easy to spot: never borrow money to buy stocks — and I mean never! If the stock goes down, you'll be paying interest on a loan to buy an asset that has lost value. One of the most common forms of this behavior is 'buying on the margin,' which is the practice of borrowing money from a brokerage house to buy stocks. When a brokerage loans you money to buy stocks, you must put up collateral to guarantee repayment of the loan. The collateral consists of the stocks you bought, other stocks in your portfolio, and even your personal assets. If the value of the stock bought with borrowed money becomes less than the amount that you owe, the brokerage will make a margin call, or ask to have more money added to your account. If you don't have sufficient funds, the brokerage has the right to sell your personal assets. That includes your home, your car, and everything that contributes to your net worth.

This was commonplace during the Great Depression. Beginning in 1929, many "rich" investors who built up large portfolios with borrowed money lost everything and had to declare bankruptcy. Don't let that be you. Buying stocks with borrowed money — even if it's money from your bank — is no different than going to the casino and putting a wad of cash on 'red.' You are an investor — not a gambler.

Buying on a Tip

Buying on a tip means purchasing a stock based on insider information. There are a number of reasons why you should avoid this type of behavior. For starters, it's illegal. If everyone could buy on a tip, the market would become a very unfair place, as the pals of powerful CEOs and market movers would have an advantage over the general public. Secondly, tips can be unreliable. Officers of a company announce future expectations in a public manner; they never divulge such information to an outside group or individual. Most of the time, so-called 'tips' are nothing more than rumors meant to hype a stock. Remember that there aren't any shortcuts in the world of investing. Cheating won't lead to success!

Selling Short

Selling short flips everything that we've studied on its head. Rather than scouting for low-priced stocks and hoping that they will rise, the short seller looks for high-priced stocks and hoping for them to drop. This is akin to betting against the market, which follows a historically upward trend.

When an investor sells short, he borrows a stock from a brokerage with the anticipation that the price will drop. The investor doesn't own that stock; he has merely borrowed it and passed it along to another investor. If the investor guesses correctly and the price indeed drops, he or she can buy shares of the stock at the depressed price to replace the borrowed shares. The investor will end up profiting from the difference between the amount paid for the borrowed shares and the depressed price.

But if the investor guesses wrong and the price of the stock goes up — and there's no limit on how high a stock may go — the seller will ultimately have to buy back the stock at the increased price. In this case, the investor loses money, as he borrowed shares worth less than what he ended up buying them for. The brokerage has the right to call for the short sale to be 'covered,' at which the investor has to accept his or her loss. You may have heard the term 'short squeeze'; this happens when a group of large investors pump up a stock so the short sellers have to cover their positions, a costly event.

If you dig more into selling short, you'll realize that it's more than risky. It's a pretty slimy practice to bet on financial failure.

Foreign Sovereign Bonds

Sovereign bonds are bonds issued by and backed by a given country. All of the bonds that we've discussed so far are United States sovereign bonds. But buying sovereign bonds issued by foreign countries pose two risks: 1) the currency exchange rate is subject to change; and 2) countries can default. The first risk can be lessened by buying bonds that are sold and redeemed in U.S. dollars — not the issuing country's currency. These are called dollar-denominated bonds. But there's no avoiding the second risk. If you think that it's rare for countries to default, you're mistaken. Over the past thirty years, over 20 countries have defaulted, including Russia. In each of those cases, the holders of sovereign bonds in the failing country lost most of their investment.

Commodity Trading

Trading in commodities means that you aren't investing in a company; you're investing in the goods that a company uses to conduct its operations. There are four basic types of commodities:

- Metals (silver, gold, etc)
- Energy (oil, natural gas, etc)
- Livestock (hogs, cattle, etc)

- Agriculture (corn, fruit, etc)

When you trade in an energy commodity, for example, you aren't buying a company like Chevron; you're buying a contract for so many barrels of oil. If you don't sell the contract prior to expiration, you might find barrels of oil on your front lawn, or a bunch of hogs if you bought a contract on the price of swine and forgot to sell. Another downside is that commodity contracts are highly-leveraged, so small movements in price can cause large profits or losses. Stick to what you know and forget about commodities.

Hedge Funds

A hedge fund is a partnership of investors that invests in stocks and bonds using strategies such as short selling and leverage. They also invest in assets such as real estate, bullion (gold bars), and currencies. Because hedge funds invest in assets other than stocks and bonds, they are not regulated by the market. There are also limitations as to who can join a hedge fund. While some can be considerably successful, they pose glaring risks to the investor. A quick example: Long Term Capital Management (LTCM) was a large hedge fund that was led by Nobel Prize winners and renowned investors. It figured out a way to make big bets with a supposed "low-risk" strategy. That "low risk" became a reality, and LTCM went bankrupt.

Initial Public Offering (IPO)

An Initial Public Offering (IPO) is when a private company decides to "go public," raising capital by selling shares to stockholders. When a new company decides to go public, I suggest waiting a beat and seeing which way the wind blows before buying shares. Why, you might ask? I have two good reasons for you.

First of all, you have to pay a premium in order to invest in an IPO. When a new company goes public, it sells shares to an underwriter at an initial price. Then, the underwriter resells those shares, first to clients and insiders, and then to the public after a markup. Aside from the premium, IPOs attract lots of hype and expectation, which typically inflates the value of each share.

Second, many companies are losing money when they first go public, and it's impossible to know how they're going to perform in the long run. Many people who buy new companies do so because they're generating buzz on the internet, or because they're thinking about the needles in the haystack that have hit it big.

There you have it — we've exposed all of the monsters in the closet. While I strongly discourage pursuing any of these investments, I should note that they don't always fail. Throughout your investing career, you're bound to hear about people who strike gold on an IPO or a hedge fund. Don't let these particular success stories knock you off of your course. As long-term investors, we aren't looking for a flash in the pan. We're looking for steady gains that span the course of decades.

/

The 6 Bear Markets

Just like individual stocks, the collective market can drop quickly and unexpectedly. Sometimes, down markets, or bear markets can last a few days, and on other occasions, they can last for years. I want to introduce you to the six bear markets of the past forty years. These economic downturns offer valuable insight into the dips that are bound to happen in the future.

A bear market that has since been known as "Black Monday" occurred on October 19, 1987. Without any precipitating news event, the market lost 20% of its value, which is the greatest one-day percentage drop in U.S. market history. Most economists agree that the cause of Black Monday was investor panic; people became nervous that prices were rising too high, resulting in multiple stockholders cashing out their stocks all at once. This produced a domino effect; plummeting stock prices scared more people into selling their shares, which further decreased prices. The market remained down for over 3 months and ultimately lost 33% of value from its previous high, as measured by the S&P 500 index.

During the late 1990s and early 2000s, stock of Internet companies became the darlings of the stock market. In what came to be known as the 'Dot-Com Bubble,' investors ran up the prices of these stocks based on expectation, not on earnings. The bubble eventually burst in October 2001, and the crash continued to October 2002. During the crash, the market went down 78%, and many companies went out of business.

The market lost over 50% of its value during the economic recession that began in late-2007 and lasted until early-2009. I've referred to this disaster throughout this book; it was the result of a real estate boom where lenders issued mortgages to people who could not afford the debt. This practice of subprime lending was motivated by the greed of the banks, who wanted to recoup extra high interest rates from clients who weren't financially equipped to put down-payments on homes. It ended up backfiring when people defaulted on their mortgages. Although the bear market ended in 2009, it took 5 years for the market to return to its pre-crash level. Thereafter, the economy continued to rise to all-time heights. This bear market wasn't caused by changes in industry, economic policy, or international events. Rather, it was caused by domestic banking practices and reckless investors who thought they could flip houses and make a quick profit. While it had a devastating effect on the economy, the market recovered as per usual.

On May 6, 2010, the market experienced a 'flash crash,' dropping almost 1,000 points within minutes before partially recovering. The cause has been attributed to program trading by large funds. In program trading, large financial institu-

tions program their computers to buy or sell based on information that the computer receives. When several powerful
institutions get the same mandate to sell all at once, it can
have a severe impact on the economy.

From May 2011 to October 2011 the market dropped 21%. The
plummet was precipitated by a sovereign debt crisis that
started in Greece and spread to Spain and Italy. A debt crisis
is when a country owes so much money and doesn't have the
resources to pay what it owes, much like a company experi-
encing bankruptcy. Countries that owe a lot of money often
begin printing more money to pay off their debt, but that
weakens the value of their currency and makes the crisis
worse. In 2011, the fear was that Greece, Spain, and Italy
might default on their debt and their financial woes might
spread to other countries, seriously affecting the U.S. markets.
The lesson to be learned from the 2011 financial crisis is that
we live in a worldwide economy. What happens in a far
corner of the world can still affect our stock market.

The last bear market of recent memory occurred between
September 2018 and December 24, 2018 when the market
dropped 20%. This crash was precipitous and brief in
comparison to prior bear markets. The sell-off was thought to
be motivated by concern that the Fed would raise rates and
that the profit could not be maintained. By January 2019, the
market recovered.

Interspaced between these bear markets were smaller market
declines. After every drop, the market has ultimately
rebounded and reached a new high. History has shown that

dips in the stock market are an inevitability. I say this to prepare you for the morning when you find that the value of your investment portfolio has plummeted. This is never a good feeling, but it's to be expected: every long-term investor will go through periods of loss. Overall, have faith in the U.S. economy and the market: it will steadily rise over time and bail you out.

The Flag is Up: The Ideal Portfolio

When every racehorse is lined up in the starting gate, an official called "the starter" raises a flag. Then there's an internal announcement: "the flag is up." This means that all of the entrants are prepared and ready for the race to commence. It isn't until the starter drops his flag that the gates fly open and the horses burst down the track.

Having made it to the end of this book, you're like a horse in the starting gate. You've assimilated the knowledge to help you become a successful investor, and you're now ready to start your investing career that will lead to wealth at the time of retirement.

Before dropping the flag, I want to offer some ideas about a suggested portfolio. Take this as food for thought and something to hang your hat on. A necessary disclaimer: the market is forever changing, which means that you should take my thoughts with a grain of salt. Companies that are the bluebloods today may become laggards tomorrow. Look no further than companies like U.S. Steel and General Electric, which were considered some of the safest investments you could make just a few decades ago. Today, they're in the back row. Alternatively, new and undiscovered technologies may set the stage for unexpected stars in the future. Facebook and Apple didn't exist when I started my investing career; today, they're blockbusters. This is all to say that you must keep up-to-date on the ever-changing market environment. Additionally, individuals have different investment personalities. What may be an ideal portfolio for one investor may not suit another. Notwithstanding the above, I'll outline my prototype for an ideal portfolio and then mention some companies that I deem promising for investment.

As discussed earlier, diversification should be the safety net of your investment portfolio. Never put all of your eggs in one basket. The ideal portfolio should have a primary investment, or anchor. The remainder of the portfolio should be diversified to include:

- A collection of 10-30 different companies
- An even contribution to your holdings
- Companies in several economic sectors
- A balance of value stocks and growth stocks
- A dark horse

The anchor of your portfolio.

Before you spread your wings and begin buying individual companies, I recommend establishing an anchor. This investment will serve as the mainstay of your portfolio, and you will continually add shares regardless of whether the market is up or down. Your anchor should be an index fund that mirrors the market. You can probably guess which two I'm about to suggest: the S&P 500 (SPY) and the Dow Jones Industrial Average (DIA). Both are smart selections; I personally suggest the S&P 500 because it includes 500 companies as opposed to the 30 of the Dow Jones Industrial Average. By selecting an index fund as your anchor, you're betting that the economy and the stock market will prosper over time. History has shown that this is a smart bet to make.

What percentage of your portfolio should you dedicate to your anchor? That really depends on your investment temperament and your tolerance for risk. If you're conservative and don't want to bother picking individual companies, you should put the lion's share or even the entirety of your funds into an established index fund. However, if you're interested in hand-picking individual companies that might explode, you could dedicate as little as 10% of your portfolio to your anchor. Regardless of what you choose to do, kick off your portfolio with your anchor investment.

The number of companies in your portfolio.

The number of companies that you hold will ebb and flow over the course of your career. You'll own just a few companies when you get started, but that number will grow over time. The ideal number that you should shoot for is between 10 and 30. Investing in fewer than 10 companies puts your portfolio at risk if one or two should go sour, and it's difficult to keep up-to-date on more than 30 companies.

Spreading the dollars invested.

Beyond your anchor, the dollar amounts of your portfolio should be spread evenly among individual companies. This strategy ensures that your portfolio is properly diversified. Because the price per share of each company will vary, spreading your dollars will mean fewer shares in expensive companies and more shares in cheaper ones.

Balancing holdings among economic sectors.

As I noted in Chapter 1, the stock market is divided into 11 economic sectors that rarely go in the same direction or at the same rate over a given period of time. Since you cannot predict which sectors will rise and which sectors will fall, you need to own companies in several sectors. That's a major part of spreading risk.

Value and growth stocks.

In addition to spreading your individual companies among economic sectors, you'll want to balance your portfolio between value stocks and growth stocks. Recall that value stocks are safer investments that tend to be more expensive, whereas growth stocks are riskier but potentially yield higher returns. Value stocks tend to have lower PE ratios, close to the historic norm of 15, and growth stocks have much higher PEs. The ratio between value and growth stocks is somewhat arbitrary and will vary depending on your preference for risk. If you want to be safer, select more value stocks. If you're feeling more daring, you might want to weigh your portfolio with more growth stocks.

Choosing a dark horse.

Once you have your anchor and your satellite investments in place, I recommend buying the occasional high-risk investment that has great potential. You shouldn't count on seeing this money again, but it could very well explode. Just don't go overboard. You have an investment plan; don't veer too far off course.

Once you begin investing, you must keep your garden growing. Contribute to your portfolio regardless of the fluctuating market, add shares using dollar averaging, and place all dividend-paying stocks in a dividend reinvestment program. If one stock has a strange spike and seems to be selling for more than you think it's worth, sell half and put that money into a new investment. The key is to keep adding to your portfolio over time.

/

Companies to Consider

I've already offered two recommendations for your anchor; now, I'll suggest some interesting companies in different sectors of the market. While these are my favorites in today's economy, they may not be yours. Before being trigger-happy and buying these companies, do your research and make your own decisions.

Value Stocks

JPMorgan Chase (JPM). JPM is in the financial sector, has a PE of 13 and pays a 2.6% dividend. Jamie Diamond is the CEO and is considered one of the smartest bankers in the business. Good management means a well-run company.

Caterpillar (CAT). Caterpillar is a giant of the Industrial sector, manufacturing heavy-duty equipment used in mining and construction. If you pass a construction site, you'll likely see yellow construction vehicles with the company's logo: CAT. With the government committed to repairing the country's infrastructure, bridges, and highways, Caterpillar's equipment should be in demand. With a PE of 14 and a yield just under 3%, Caterpillar is a stable and conservative investment.

Apple (AAPL). Apple is one of my favorites in the Technology sector. The iPhone is the #1 mobile phone sold in the United States, accounting for about 45% of the market. In addition to the iPhone, Apple sells computers, tablets, and smart watches. In 2019, it started branching into television. It sells at a PE of 24, slightly on the high side for value, and has a 1% dividend.

Berkshire Hathaway (BRK-A or BRK-B). Berkshire Hathaway has long been considered one of the great companies. Berkshire has two classes of shares: Class A (BRK-A) and Class B (BRK-B). The A shares are selling for over $30,000, while the B shares are hovering around $200. Let's stick with the B shares. Berkshire owns or has a large position in a number of companies. To that extent, it's like a mutual fund. With Berkshire you're putting your money with the guru of Wall Street: Warren Buffett. It isn't a bad idea to bet on Buffett.

Growth Stocks

Amazon (AMZN). Amazon is considered to be within the Consumer Discretionary sector, but it's becoming a lot more. While Amazon's PE of 79 makes it a bit of a risk, everyone I know, including myself, buys products through Amazon. Over the past 5 years, Amazon's revenue has gone from $107 billion to $265 billion, which accounts for the high PE. The amazing thing about Amazon is that it doesn't have any real competitors at the moment. If you want a growth stock, you can't do better than Amazon.

Costco (COST). Costco falls within the Consumer Staple sector. Costco has a fabulous business model. By last count, it has over 90 million customers, and the cost of membership begins at $60. That adds up to $5.4 billion before they open the door. A PE of 34 puts it in the growth category.

Dividend Stock

Enterprise Products Partners (EPD). At some point along the way, you'll want to incorporate stocks that pay a good dividend for your retirement account. Enterprise Products Partners is a MLP that has increased its dividend every quarter since 2011. At the time of this writing, the dividend is at 6.3%, and it could go even higher. Don't expect EPD's stock price to increase much, as it pays most of its income to the stockholders as dividends.

Dark Horse

Tesla (TSLA). Tesla is a high-risk company that has a good chance of hitting it big. Tesla's red flag is that it doesn't have any earnings, which means no cash flow and plenty of risk. On the other hand, Tesla has revolutionized the automobile market with its electric cars. Tesla is the leader in sales of electric cars and probably has the best technology.

As You Get Older

As you transition from a new investor to an established investor, you'll need to rebalance your portfolio in preparation for retirement. That means taking less risk and incorporating more conservative investments. This rebalancing will include a tilt toward value stocks and fixed income securities. Revisit Chapter 7 for everything you need to know about fixed income securities, but consider the following principles:

- Add stocks that pay a stable dividend. Preferred stocks and MLPs are a great idea.

- Invest in certificates of deposit (CDs) if you are searching for a safe, short-term investment (a few months to 2 years). You can also use United States Bills through the Treasury Department for short-term investments, but CDs usually pay a better interest rate.

- Invest in United State Notes if you're looking for a maturity term from 2 to 5 years.

- Invest in bonds or bond funds for investments longer than 5 years.

- Consider seeking a bond specialist to select and buy your bonds.

- If you decide to self-manage your bond portfolio, buy tax-free municipal bonds (general obligation bonds are particularly safe) and stagger the maturities between 5 and 10 years.

To get the maximum benefit from tax-free municipal bonds, buy ones that are issued from the state in which you live.

- For your IRA or tax-deferred retirement account, buy corporate and taxable municipal bonds with maturities between 5 and 10 years. Always buy bonds of investment quality, and stay away from junk bonds.

/

Parting Remarks

Congratulations: you're now well-equipped to become a successful investor! Now that you have all of the knowledge to make a killing, I'd like to leave you with a few sentiments that I wish I had heard when I was starting out. First and foremost, remain disciplined and keep your eye on your goal: a comfortable retirement. Along the way, expect to make investments that lose money. This happens to everyone; no one bats 1.000. When losses occur, sell your holdings and move on without getting discouraged. Take solace in the fact that you have a long-term plan, and stick with it.

And now, I'll give you the most important advice to becoming a successful investor: do your own research, make your own decisions, and carry the strength of your convictions.

EPILOGUE

On my grandson Jacob's 13th birthday, after we sang "Happy Birthday" and he opened his presents, I asked him about his investments. He told me that he owns two shares of Apple, one share of Microsoft, and of course one share of the S&P 500.

"Those are good investments," I said. "What made you want to buy them?"

"I bought Apple because I have an iPhone, Microsoft because it makes the XBox, and the S&P 500 because you told me it's the best investment that I could make."

Not a bad answer. The two of us went on to look at the performance of his small yet promising portfolio. Apple was up 27%, Microsoft was up 7%, and the S&P 500 was up 18%.

When I asked Jacob if he had sold any stocks, Jacob replied

that he bought and sold one share of Costco, which gave him a small profit.

"Why did you sell?" I asked.

"The stock price had barely moved."

I went on to explain that the stock price of a good company doesn't always go up. But over time, investing in a well-run company will reward you. Jacob and I made an agreement: he wouldn't sell a stock without first calling me and explaining his reasoning, and I wouldn't tell him to sell or not to sell.

Before I left, Jacob told me that he was taking a finance class as an elective. A great idea!

Move over Mr. Buffet: Jacob is coming.

GLOSSARY

Anchor — the primary investment of your portfolio, ideally one of the established index funds.

Annual Report — a report that includes a wealth of information on a public company's yearly performance. I recommend reading the "Report to Shareholders" within this document.

Ask Price — the amount of money for which a person is willing to sell his/her shares of stock.

Assets — everything of value that a company owns. Tangible assets have established values, whereas intangible assets do not have established values.

Balance Sheet — a financial document that lists a company's Assets and Liabilities.

Bear Market — a term used to describe a market that is

decreasing. A true bear market is a loss of at least 20% from the previous high and persists for 2 months.

Beta Value — a measure of a stock's volatility. When beta is greater than '1,' the company is more volatile than the market; when beta is less than '1,' the company is less volatile than the market.

Bid Price — the amount of money for which a person is willing to buy shares of stock.

Bond — a fixed income security in which the investor 'loans' money to a borrower (a corporation or municipality).

Bond Credit Rating — a way of evaluating a bond's credibility. Major agencies rate bonds on a scale of AAA (triple A) to BBB- (triple B minus).

Bond Fund — a fund that invests your money into a pool of different bonds. Bond funds are professionally managed and do not require the investor to contribute in lots of $1,000.

Book Value — a measurement of how much a company is actually worth. Book value is calculated by finding the assets of a company minus its liabilities.

Book Value per Share (BVPS) — what the owner of a stock would receive for each share if the company were sold and the assets were equally distributed to shareholders.

Bottom-Up Approach — using the success of one company to unearth other fruitful companies in a similar industry.

Bull Market — a term used to describe a market that is increasing.

Brokerage house aka Brokerage — a middle-man business that has a relationship with stock exchanges and manages your transactions in the stock market.

Call — the right to buy a stock at a predetermined price (the strike price) within a specified time (the exercise date).

Call Provision — a stipulation that allows bond issuers to buy back the bond before the maturity date.

Capital — a sum of assets that are required for investment. For your purposes, capital refers to cash, but it also includes assets that hold financial value.

Capital Gains Rate — the tax rate that applies to profits made from long-term investments (over 1 year). The capital gains rate is lower than the ordinary rate.

Cash Flow Statement — a financial document that indicated the money that a company receives from its business, investments, and other sources of income minus Liabilities.

Certificates of Deposit (CDs) — a fixed-income security that produces interest without posing risk to the investor. The money from a CD cannot be accessed until the investment reaches maturity.

Checking Account — a bank account that includes your spending money.

Commodity Trading — an investment that centers on the

goods that a company uses to conduct its operations rather than the company itself. Trading commodities is not recommended for the novice investor.

Compounding — a strategy in which the investor reinvests interest or dividends so that future interest or dividends will be based on the accumulated amount. Compounding works especially well in a Tax-Deferred Retirement Account.

Consumer Price Index (CPI) — a metric that is largely used to determine the country's inflation rate.

Convertible Preferred — a marker indicating that the investor can convert preferred shares into common shares.

Coupon Rate — a percentage that corresponds to a preferred stocks' dividend. Look for high numbers.

Cumulative Preferred — a marker indicating that if the dividend of a preferred stock is eliminated but later restored, the company must reimburse the investor for all dividends that have been held back.

CUSIP Number — a number that identifies individual bonds. The CUSIP allows you to research different interest rates, call provisions, and maturity dates for a given bond sold through different brokerages.

Discount Brokerage — a type of brokerage that allows you to carry out your transactions without professional guidance.

Diversification — a strategy through which you can offset risk by investing in different types of investments in a variety of economic sectors.

Dividends — an amount of money that company management distributes to shareholders for each share of stock owned. Usually distributed on a quarterly basis.

Dividend Reinvestment Program (DRP) — a program that allows you to compound the value of your dividends by reinvesting them to buy additional shares of the issuing company.

Dividend Yield — how the dividend of a stock compares to the price per share. Yield is the chief metric to monitor if you're buying a stock for its dividend.

Dollar Cost Averaging — an investment strategy in which the investor commits to a sum to invest and a set interval at which that investment will occur.

Dow Jones Industrial Average Index Fund (DIA) — one of the main index funds that tracks the performance of the collective market. The DIA fund should be a pillar of your investment portfolio.

Earnings — a company's revenue minus the the costs of running business.

Earnings per Share (EPS) — how much a company earns for every share outstanding. High values indicate that a company has a healthy cash flow.

Economic Sectors — categories of the economy that are used to classify different types of businesses.

Ex-Dividend Date — the date on which shares are traded without the prior dividend.

Exchange Traded Fund (ETF) — a fund that spreads one's investments across an array of companies in a specific industry or field. ETFs allow the investor to bank on an industry as opposed to an individual company.

Expense Ratio — a fund's cost of doing business, which is passed onto investors regardless of the fund's performance.

The Federal Reserve (The Fed) — the United States' banking system, which monitors the economy by regulating monetary policy and the federal funds rate.

Fixed Income — a type of security that produces steady, predictable returns to the investor. It is advised to incorporate fixed income securities into one's portfolio over time to protect against risk.

Float — see "Shares Outstanding."

Foreign Sovereign Bonds — bonds that are issued and backed by countries outside of the United States. Investing in Foreign Sovereign Bonds is not recommended for the novice investor because exchange rates are subject to change and countries can default.

Full-Service Brokerage — a type of brokerage that provides you with access to financial professionals and additional resources. As such, they have higher associated fees.

Good Will — what a company considers their name to be worth. We can interpret this as an intangible asset because the exact value is up to interpretation.

Growth Stock — stocks that have the high potential to increase their value in years to come. In exchange, they also pose more risk.

Halving the Double — a strategy in which the investor sells half of his/her shares that have recently spiked upward, using the cash to reinvest elsewhere. This ensures that you still have equity in the "hot" company while protecting you from sudden drops.

Hedge Funds — a partnership of investors that deal with stocks, bonds, real estate, bullion, and many other types of assets. Investing in hedge funds is not recommended for the amateur investor.

Herd Effect — a misguided motivation of buying stocks in which a person makes an investment based on the actions of other people.

Income Statement — a financial document that lists a company's Revenue and Earnings/Income.

Index Fund — a fund that offsets risk by spreading one's investment across a wide array of companies.

Individual Retirement Account (IRA) — a type of retirement account that you can set up in addition to the accounts provided by your employer.

Inflation — the ongoing loss of money's buying power over time. Inflation is the reason why prices increase from year-to-year.

Inflation Rate — the percent increase of goods & services from one year to the next.

Initial Public Offering (IPO) — when a company that is privately-owned decides to "go public," opening up its shares to the stock market. Investing in companies that have recently IPO'd is not recommended.

K1 Form — a tax form that is issued by any partnership.

Large Cap Stock — a company with a market value of more than $1 billion.

Liabilities — everything that a company owes, such as loans and other financial obligations.

Limit Order — a type of stock transaction in which you can stipulate a set price at which you will buy or sell a given stock. If the stock reaches that price, the transaction will be processed automatically for you.

Load — an unnecessary fee, expressed as a percentage, that is tacked onto some open mutual funds.

Long-Term Investing — a strategy that minimizes the risks of stocks by relying on the upward trend of the market. Long-term investing requires the investor to hold onto his/her investment for the long haul, unless specific criteria merit otherwise.

Lots — the $1,000 increments in which the investor can buy bonds.

Master Limited Partnership (MLP) — a type of fixed-income security that produces healthy dividends for the investor.

Momentum Investing — when a person buys a stock just because the price is going up. Don't fall into this trap!

Mutual Fund — a hands-off type of investment that pools your dollars into a fund that is managed by a professional manager.

MRQ — most recent quarter.

NASDAQ Stock Exchange (NASDAQ) — another major stock exchange, where traders operate through a dealer.

Net Asset Value — a metric that indicates what a company is actually worth. The Net Asset Value is found by subtracting a company's Liabilities from its Assets.

Net Asset Value per Share (NAV/Share) — the amount that one shareholder would receive for each share if the assets were equally distributed to all the shareholders.

New York Stock Exchange (NYSE) — one of the most prominent stock exchanges.

Options — a risky investment that includes 'puts' and 'calls.' Option trading is not recommended for the novice investor.

Ordinary Rate — the tax rate that applies to profits made from short-term investments (less than 1 year). The ordinary rate is higher than the capital gains rate.

Par — the face value of a bond, to which the price of a bond should be compared.

Portfolio — your collection of investments, including stocks, exchange-traded funds, index funds, and other types of financial securities.

Preferred Stock — a stock that has a fixed dividend and set dates on which those dividends will be paid.

Price/Book — a measure of how much book value you receive for buying a share of stock. Look for numbers less than '1.'

Price/Earning Ratio (P/E) — a measurement that determines how well a stock is priced. P/E is calculated by dividing the price per share by the earnings per share.

Price/Share — the going price of one share of stock.

Principal (Bond) — the amount of money that a bondholder receives when the bond reaches maturity.

Program Trading — the practice of using sophisticated computer programs to buy and sell stocks based on reams of data.

Proposal — questions faced by public companies on which shareholders can vote at annual meetings or by proxy using a computer.

Proxy battle — a leadership standoff for a public company, where shareholders can vote on which group is best equipped to run the business.

Put — the right to sell a stock at a predetermined price (the strike price) within a specified time (the exercise date).

Record Date — the date on which you must be listed as a shareholder to be eligible to receive a dividend.

Return on Equity (ROE) — a percentage that represents how profitable a company is in relation to its equity. ROE measures how well a company has increased its profits.

Revenue — the amount that a company makes through its business.

Roth IRA — a type of IRA in which the investor pays taxes on contributions; not when funds are withdrawn.

Shares Outstanding (aka the Float) — The majority of a public company's shares, which are released to be traded on the stock market.

S&P 500 Index Fund (SPY) — one of the main index funds that tracks the performance of the collective market. The SPY fund should be a pillar of your investment portfolio.

Savings Account — a bank account that includes the money set aside in case of emergencies or unanticipated expenditures.

Selling Short — an inverted investment in which the investor looks for stocks that are going to drop. Selling short is not recommended for the novice investor.

Small Cap Stock — a company with a market value of less than $1 billion.

Stock Dividends — dividends that are distributed as shares of stock as opposed to cash.

Stock Exchange — organizations through which investors can buy and sell shares of stock.

Structured Products — a technical investment that requires the investor to gamble on interest rates. Buying structured products is not recommended for the novice investor.

Taxable Investing Account — the account that includes your portfolio of investments. The funds in your taxable investing account can be accessed at any time.

Tax-Deferred Retirement Account — the account that includes the investments that you're making for retirement. These funds cannot be accessed until you reach the age of 59 ½.

Top-Down Approach — using the success of an industry to find individual companies that are worth investing in.

Traditional IRA — a type of IRA in which the investor pays taxes when funds are withdrawn; not when the investor contributes up-front.

Treasury Inflation Protected Securities (TIPS) (Treasuries) — a type of treasury that is designed to guard the investor from inflation. The interest received from TIPS varies with respect to the rate of inflation.

TTM — trailing twelve months

United States Treasuries — a fixed-income security in which the individual loans money to the government. Treasuries guarantee interest payments and are exempt from local and state taxes.

United States Bills (Treasuries) — a type of short-term treasury that reaches maturity between 4 weeks and 1 year.

United States Notes (Treasuries) — a type of mid-term treasury that reaches maturity between 1 and 10 years.

Value Stock — stocks that are considered to be stable, risk-averse, and established in their business.

YOY — year after year.

Yield to Maturity (YTM) — a rate that anticipates the investor's total return on a bond if it's held to maturity.

Yield to Call (YTC) — a rate that anticipates the investor's total return on a bund if it's called before maturity.

52-Week High & Low — the highest and lowest price per share of a stock over the past year. This reflects the volatility of a stock's price.

ACKNOWLEDGMENTS

As I've written, this project began when my grandson Jacob asked me how to invest in the stock market. I enjoyed teaching throughout my career as a surgeon, so explaining investing concepts was enjoyable and came easily to me. It soon became apparent that Jacob's ability to grasp the subject matter went far beyond what I had anticipated, and I decided to record the major aspects of investing for Jacob and others who want to seize control of their financial future.

While I've authored numerous scientific articles and chapters in textbooks, I had never written material beyond my specialty of vascular surgery. I needed help and encouragement to take on this project, validate the information, and present the concepts in a way that would be clear and interesting to read. The following people were essential in helping me with those objectives and bringing the project to fruition.

Aaron Eshman, a former executive at Morgan Stanley. Bunny edited my early manuscript. provided critical feedback, and encouraged me throughout the publishing process. Words do not adequately express my appreciation to Bunny.

Lawrence Sternshein, C.P.A. Larry offered key insights and fact-checked my statements about taxation of investments. He did his review during "Tax Time," which placed a burden on him and was greatly appreciated by me.

Gary Fournier, Managing Director and Financial Advisor at J. P. Morgan Securities. Gary reviewed my final draft and provided valuable advice. I deeply appreciate Gary taking time from his busy schedule, and it was an honor to get his notes.

My editor, Nick Katleman. Nick took my initial manuscript and showed me how to rearrange the topics and present the information in a more enjoyable way for the reader. Without his expertise, this book would never have been published.

My four children — Deborah, Gerald, Robert, and Michael. My children gave me unwavering support throughout this journey, and I'll always be grateful to them. It's comforting to have your family behind you when you're embarking on a new venture.

My ten grandchildren, who encouraged me throughout the writing process and helped me through one of the most diffi-cult parts of writing a book: selecting a title!

My wife Bette, without whose ongoing support I would have never started or completed this project.